THE RELUCTANT PILGRIM

Buen Camino!

Bruce Carino

Paul Haselden

Also by this author:

Seven Humor Habits for Workplace Wellness
(30-minute video DVD)

Mt. Fuji: The Fool Climbs It Twice
(30-minute video DVD)

PAUL HUSCHILT

THE
RELUCTANT PILGRIM

AN INCOMPLETE GUIDE TO WALKING
THE CAMINO DE SANTIAGO

SIGNAN PRESS

The Reluctant Pilgrim:
An Incomplete Guide to Walking the Camino de Santiago

Signan Press
Toronto, Ontario, Canada

Library and Archives Canada Cataloguing in Publication

Huschilt, Paul

The reluctant pilgrim : an incomplete guide to walking the
Camino de Santiago / Paul Huschilt.

ISBN 978-0-9735450-1-2

1. Huschilt, Paul—Travel—Spain—Santiago de Compostela—
Humor. 2. Santiago de Compostela (Spain)—Description and
travel—Humor. 3. Christian pilgrims and pilgrimages—Spain—
Santiago de Compostela—Humor. I. Title.

DP402.S23H88 2011   914.6'11   C2011-906786-2

Written by: Paul Huschilt
Illustrations by: Paul Huschilt
Editor: Philip Fine
Cover and text design: David Vereschagin, Quadrat Communications
Back cover photo: DSTFotografie, www.DSTFotografie.de.to
Author photo: Joel Drutz

Visit www.paulhuschilt.com

Visit www.thereluctantpilgrim.com

Printed in Canada

MIX
Paper from
responsible sources
FSC
www.fsc.org
FSC® C016245

For Kevin, who walked with me these 19 years

and with gratitude to my parents,
for everything else.

CONTENTS

ACKNOWLEDGEMENTS

First and foremost, I want to thank my two dear friends who walked the Camino de Santiago with me across northern Spain. Without these amazing women, the adventure of writing this book would not have taken place. I am forever grateful for their tenacity, planning, humour, charm and fun. Most of all, I am indebted to them for allowing me to write about our experiences, using the pseudonyms of Rita Lawrence and Fujiko Yokohama to protect their privacy.

Special thanks to all those who read excerpts or first drafts and provided feedback, including Marie McNamee, Fusako Nakamura, Hiromi Hajikano, Susanne Wussow, Kevin McEvenue, Adele Alfano, Pat Harper, Sandra Paquette, Colleen Clarke, Monika Strak, Christina Prozes, Lynn Davies, Eve Davies-Greenwald, Susan Sweeney, Eileen Pease, Dianne McCoy, Sean McEvenue, Carole Cameron, Judith Heilizer, Karen Whalen, Maryvon Delanoë, Maki Miyake and Jennifer Moore.

My editor Philip Fine helped me eliminate 30,000 words from the original manuscript. For that, I owe him a debt of gratitude, and come to think of it, so do you. Without his brave cuts, the Incomplete guide would never have been written. I'm grateful to him as well for his astute and clear direction. It's been a journey and an absolute pleasure. Thanks.

Special thanks, too, to my clients and to the more than 100,000 people who have watched me perform as a professional speaker. You've allowed me to do what I love most – to spread joy by encouraging people to laugh, think and focus on wellness. Your indulgence over the last 11 years has transformed my life and world view. Thank you.

And to the millions of people who have walked the Camino over the 1,200 years of its existence, I both thank you and blame you for the inspiration.

DISCLAIMER

I've always wanted to write an incomplete guide to something, and here it is – as half-baked as I've dared to make it. And yet, I felt it wouldn't be unabridged enough if it didn't include this small disclaimer.

As much as I have tried to provide an accurate, albeit humorous, account of walking the traditional Christian pilgrimage called the Camino de Santiago de Compostela, there are a couple of things you should know. Day 7 was not as sunny as I say, while Day 17 was not as uniformly grey. Looking back, the rain on Day 22 was not as bad, while the rain on Day 23 was worse. We really did do laundry every night, but not everything on the last day was quite as sturdy as I describe. Don't say I didn't warn you.

I also changed the names of people I wrote about so they couldn't sue the pants off me.

Other than that, what I write about is exactly how it happened … more or less.

It's time to move along now, pilgrim.

Enjoy the walk.

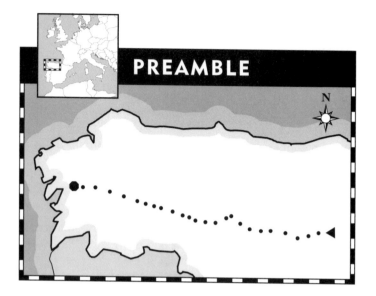

IT'S HARD TO SAY when a pilgrimage begins in earnest. Is it when you down two beers before getting on the plane? Is it on board the flight there? From the first day of walking? Or is it much earlier than that? Like when you decide to go? Or, in my case, does it begin only when I finally stop resisting and enter the experience wholeheartedly?

As I ruminated, Train 203 from Madrid to Burgos shook its way into the Cantabrian Mountains. The ground stretched downward and patches of snow appeared like sand traps in an Arctic golf course. I thought about the winter coat that I had decided was too heavy to carry; I left it at the Best Western Hotel *Atlántico* in Madrid and would see it again upon our return in a month. We were to have walked 505.2 km* by then, but, in the meantime, Spain would warm up ... we hoped.

---

* If you're American, you might need to know that 505.2 km is 313.9 miles. (One mile = 1.6 km). You'll find distances in this book are always in kilometres. But don't worry. The book will read just as easily (and 1.6 times more impressively) if you simply think in miles.

Suddenly, I found myself asking the same question I always ask before setting out on once-in-a-lifetime adventures: Why am I here?

It seemed like such an easy question.

From what I could remember, the idea to walk the Catholic pilgrimage called the Camino de Santiago started on the other side of the globe, in Japan. I had been enjoying an amazing meal with my friends Amiko and Fujiko. We were seated on an outdoor terrace facing the Japanese alps after having led five weeks of wellness retreats together. We were all eager for something more.

"What next?" asked Fujiko.

"We walk the Camino!" said Amiko.

"Of course!" I exclaimed. Unfortunately, my attempt at sarcasm was lost in translation, and at that moment the path was set.

It's not that the Camino was something I was against, it was just that my impression had always been that it would be a month of walking along busy highways, eating forgettable food, sleeping in crowded hostels for a religion I no longer believed in. It was just not my cup of tea.

But then, Amiko died of cancer. I wondered if it was time to bow out. But out of respect, Fujiko wouldn't let go. "For Amiko, I walk for peace," she said.

Then it got more complicated.

Without consulting me, Fujiko invited my dear friend Rita. And although Rita and I have been through a lot together, I wasn't sure suffering across the rainiest part of Spain was such a good idea for our friendship.

On top of that, Fujiko decided we'd walk in April – a busy month for my speaking business.

To make it work, I decided I'd write this book about my experience. I was excited about that.

But then, Rita announced we'd walk only part of the Camino; she thought it was too much to attempt it all on her four-week vacation. So rather than begin in Saint-Jean-Pied-de-Port, France, the traditional starting place for the most famous branch of the Camino, we would pick up the trail 293.3 km closer to Santiago and walk only two-thirds of the way. And that's when I felt really stuck: who'd read a book about a fractional pilgrimage?

But it was too late. I was afraid that if I bailed, Rita would too. And that would dishonour not only Fujiko but my deceased friend Amiko, as well.

So here I am ... wondering why I'm here.*

OUR TRAIN STUMBLED into the medieval town of Burgos and, according to the digital display of my waterproof wristwatch, it was 1:25 p.m. The circular town is built almost entirely out of stone and is the starting point for many Camino pilgrims, as it was for us – although best-selling authors generally schlep it from the beginning. From Burgos, it is a casual 25-day stroll to the cathedral in Santiago de Compostela, where the remains of St. James the Great, one of Christ's 12 apostles, have lain in state since being carried there circa 814 A.D.

At the time that the remains of St. James were identified (and accepted by the Pope and the Emperor Charlemagne as the real deal), Santiago de Compostela rivalled even Rome as the holiest destination for anyone moseying through Christendom. Since then, millions of pilgrims have trudged their way across the countryside on traditional paths that weave a spider web of holiness across Europe. They may be overlooked by most, but to pilgrims eager to gain plenary indulgence† for their sins, these paths are sacred roads, where it's worth risking life and limb to guarantee a worry-free life in the hereafter. Clearly I hadn't planned on risking my life, but what exactly was in store for me remained a mystery.

----

* Even though it is most impressive to walk the entire 798.5 km of the "French Way", Camino pilgrims are only required to walk the last 100 km to Santiago in order to receive an officially sanctioned certificate of completion. The fact that most pilgrims walk much more than the required 100 km is a testament to something about the human condition that may or may not involve higher intelligence.

† Plenary indulgence is a fancy term for the complete and utter forgiveness of everything you've ever done wrong. If you've been naughty lately, maybe it's time to head to Spain and start walking.

In fact, mystery, from what I had gathered, was a lot of what the Camino was about. Beyond my own unanswered question of Why am I here?, there were many more conundrums associated with this Camino. First, why is St. James the guy whose bones we're walking toward and not, let's say, St. Drogo, Patron Saint of Unattractive People, or St. Barbara, Patron Saint of Fireworks, or even St. Genesius, Patron Saint of Comedians? Why are we venerating *this* apostle of Christ, James the *Greater*, and not James the *Lesser*, the shorter of the two? (Not to mention, why did Jesus insist on having two apostles named James – wasn't it needlessly confusing?) Third, whatever possessed James the Greater to leave sunnier Jerusalem in 40 A.D. in the first place, in favour of notoriously rainy northern Spain? And after that, what convinced him to return to Jerusalem in time for his own beheading? Postmortem, what possessed him to return to aqueous Galicia? And why were his remains suddenly re-discovered 770 years later by a shepherd (circa 814 A.D.), who then lugged them to Santiago?

Most importantly, why have millions of people been inspired to walk hundreds, even thousands of kilometres to visit the remains of Christ's tallest apostle? Historically, people walked to be washed of their sins. Today though, people walk for cultural, historic, adventurist, and a myriad of other reasons, few of which have anything to do with the righting of past wrongs.

The real draw of the Camino is that it gives the average, overworked and overstressed individual – who normally doesn't have enough time in a day to contemplate choices on a menu – weeks and weeks of time to ask themselves deeply personal questions such as, Why the heck am I here?

AS WE STEPPED OFF THE TRAIN, gear on our backs, we were all smiles, although mine was fake. I couldn't speak for Rita or Fujiko, but I for one felt more than a little unsure about what I had gotten myself into. We passed through the train station lounge and stepped onto the street, where we were welcomed by an inch of rain – a downpour that stopped only once we retreated back inside the station.

Yes, I was having my doubts.

But we had travelled a lot together, Rita, Fujiko and I, including climbing Mount Fuji and being stuck in a hut just below the summit for 24 hours with no running water. We had walked Manhattan top to bottom, had experienced a sunless Vancouver, had taken a train to Quebec City, and we had driven from one end of Japan to the other, averaging 50 km per hour.

We had earned our badge for communal globetrotting and were hoping to sustain it beyond the Camino.

Fujiko was the most experienced traveller, a senior citizen who could boast having climbed 100 mountains. And we shared a love for musical theatre, having both performed in *Anne of Green Gables* in our own languages. The history Rita and I had shared was more sedentary; we had worked in an insurance office together in the '90s. We had been colleagues until Rita had come to see me play Frederic in *Pirates of Penzance*. After that, she was my friend.

We emptied the contents of our backpacks to find our plastic rain ponchos and then tried to figure out how to put them on. I slid my head into the hood, and let the back of the poncho cover the pack. I knew I had it right when I looked like the Hunchback of Notre Dame. We might have looked silly but the ponchos covered everything perfectly.

We headed outside where the rain had stopped, and walked into town sealed in our own sweat.

Guidebook in hand, Rita led us along a path lined with disfigured and leafless plane trees. Their limbs stretched out of swollen joints from one side of the tiled walkway to the other. But overhead, the limbs of separate trees were actually fused together to create one giant tree eerily welcoming us into town.

Across the river, we slowly wound our way to the cathedral. Rita said it was one of Spain's finest and that it took hundreds of years to complete. It sounded interesting, but given the cold and heavy rain, I suggested we pass on visiting the church itself and head straight into its gift shop instead, thinking it housed the Municipal Pilgrim Office.

It didn't. Instead, we learned that the Municipal Pilgrim Office is exactly 1.5 km out of town, just beyond the train station where we had just come from. I looked at my fellow pilgrims hoping to find someone to blame.

Outside the cathedral, the rain had returned as snow, which Rita and Fujiko downplayed as sleet. With the bracing wind, it pelted our faces so hard it burned, so we decided to keep our heads down and risk getting lost, which was exactly what happened next.

Despite receiving surprisingly divergent views from locals on how to get to the Municipal Pilgrim Office, we miraculously found it 40 minutes later. This was a good thing because the Municipal Pilgrim Office marked the official start to our 25-day walk.

Inside, we huddled together, held our packs and awaited instructions. Sitting on church-basement-like folding chairs, I looked around and took in the pilgrim suffering, seeing that it could be mine for the next 25 days. The adjoining bedrooms boasted more bunk beds than a summer camp. The makeshift kitchen had a sink, a fridge, a hot plate, card tables and more folding chairs. Pilgrims popped in and out of the tiny foyer like actors in a tired farce that had been running too long. They loitered about as if they were waiting for a respectable time to turn in and sleep with 18 strangers until an hour before dawn when they would rise, rinse and return to the trail.

A soft-spoken man seated behind a heavy oak desk processed pilgrims with accountant-like efficiency. Whispering in German, he converted five souls from Gelsenkirchen in one go. Then he turned to us.

"Do you have your *credencials*?"* he asked.

"No," we answered in unison.

----

* Pilgrim *credencials* are like a passport, but they won't get you into a foreign country, with or without your driver's license. *Credencials* won't get you into heaven either, although they would make for an interesting conversation, smoking your last cigarette with St. Peter outside the Pearly Gates. *Credencials* are required to sleep in pilgrim hostels. The term *credencials* is used interchangeably with "pilgrim passport."

"We become pilgrims," exclaimed Fujiko, smiling, hands on hips.

"One pilgrim, one passport, one euro," said the soft-spoken man, offering a shot of what I hoped was vodka but turned out to be flavourless tea.

All you need to become a pilgrim, it turns out, is a name, country of origin, emergency contact and a one-euro coin. If you have ever turned down a call to the seminary because of the sizeable commitment, consider becoming a pilgrim – it's the fast track to holiness! The heightened status is instantaneous, while its responsibilities require only about a month's commitment. Then you can check it off your list and carry on with your unfettered secular existence. Sure, you might have to perjure yourself by signing the pilgrim's oath swearing you'll behave like a living saint from now until Santiago. But who will know if you slip up a little along the way? And how hard can it be to be a good pilgrim anyway?

As the clerk stamped my pilgrim passport, Rita poked about, appearing to be falling in love with the place. But then, what was there not to love? You got to sleep in your own numbered bunk in your own semi-private bedroom with 18 different people from 18 different countries. You got to build friendships one broken sentence at a time, then fall asleep in a space heated only by each other's dampness. In the morning, you would awake to the thrill of a cold shower before heading out in the rain, with the weight of what you brought on your back reminding you of all that you left behind, as you set off on an honest day's walk to who knows where.

When asked if I was staying the night I answered, «No saber.» ("I don't know.") What I really wanted was to spend the night in the four-star hotel next to the deserted castle on the hill overlooking Burgos. I felt a little guilty. But was I less of a saint if, rather than sleep with 18 strangers, I chose to be true to the person I love more than anyone else and go to bed by myself?

It took me exactly four seconds to decide definitively to stay at the four-star hotel. Then, Rita and I headed back into town to find food, while Fujiko stayed behind to eat some of the Japanese space-age snacks she had in her backpack. Rita and I retraced our steps, along the stone wall, across a bridge and into a tangle of ancient Spanish streets opening on a modern commercial plaza. There, we discovered a large supermarket called *Mercadona*, which I assumed meant "Our Lady of the Supermarket."

Mercadona turned out to be a big-box store where everything is in boxes and labelled in Spanish. I opened approximately 200 items before managing to find granola, salad, apples, red peppers, yogurt and raw almonds. When I walked out, I figured I must be carrying an extra four kilograms. What was I thinking?

Rita and I exchanged a *Hasta luego* (see you soon) and I headed up on my own toward my four-star hotel as its giant neon sign shone down on me: Abba Hotel – Burgos – ☆☆☆☆. I climbed the hill toward it, following its four stars as the three kings would have if Mary had immaculately conceived quadruplets.

«¡SAN PELLEGRINO!» I declared triumphantly as I entered the glass and mahogany lobby of Abba Hotel – Burgos (☆☆☆☆) and approached the young man at the reception desk. ("I am a pilgrim!")

Rather than open his arms and envelop me in a fraternal hug, he simply stared at me blankly.

«*San pellegrino*», I repeated.

«*Señor, San Pellegrino es un tipo de agua con gaz*». ("Sir, San Pellegrino is a brand of sparkling water.")

«*Usted es pe – **re** – grino*», corrected the clerk slowly, almost spelling it out for me. ("You are a pilgrim.")

«*¿No San Pellegrino?*» I asked, a little disappointed. ("I am not a brand of sparkling water?")

«*Usted es pe – **re** – grino*», he repeated, with resignation in his voice. "You are a pilgrim."

Key in hand, I dashed up three flights of stairs and entered my suite. Room 377 had its own mahogany-panelled foyer, large enough to convert pilgrims five at a time. And it had its own bedroom, which could sleep 18 but was going to, instead, sleep only me. So what if Rita and Fujiko paid only €3 (euros) for their digs? For only 88 more, I was drunk on my own floor-to-ceiling Italian marble bathroom, with enough white towels to dress a mob of ancient Romans. What to do with all this luxury but finger through a basket of miniature shampoos, mouthwash, conditioner and lotions, seated on my own bidet and facing my own porcelain throne.

The soaking tub was so big that I imagined swimming lengths. After that, I sat at my own executive desk and imagined all the people I could write letters to on stationary provided exclusively for me. I gorged myself on approximately 300 grams* of salad fresh out of the bag, yogurt in its plastic pouch, along with granola, red peppers and apples, saving the almonds entirely for another day.

The Abba Hotel – Burgos (☆☆☆☆) was so classy that even though it was completely non-smoking, Room 377 came with an ashtray and its own brand of wooden matches. Too tired to take up yet another bad habit, I got ready for bed instead.†

Room 377 was a veritable galaxy of light sources. It took me a full 10 minutes to find all the switches to turn off so I could lie in bed and contemplate the stars high above the cathedral through my wall-to-wall windows. I lay awake thinking how determined I was to get a good night's sleep on this, the last night before the trek was to begin. It took a while because I couldn't stop thinking how pleased I was with myself for having chosen to stay in a hotel.

Eventually, I did fall asleep, looking down at the old town and, in the distance, far over the rooftops, I saw the Municipal Pilgrim Office where my friends were stacked two high, hunkering down with 16 other *pellegrinos* until morning.

* Or 0.66 pounds. If you're American, you'll need to know that weight is measured in grams or kilograms in this book, and usually cited to impress. Whenever you see grams or kilograms, simply think "heavy" and you won't miss a thing.

† At the non-smoking Best Western Hotel *Atlántico* on *la Via Grande* in Madrid, rooms come with glass ashtrays with a no-smoking decal glued on the bottom. Bit of a mixed message, I'd say.

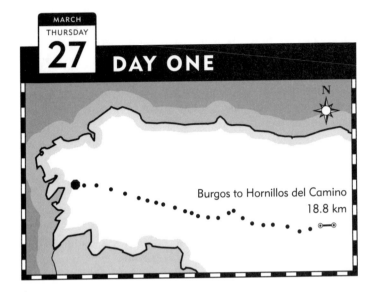

N

Burgos to Hornillos del Camino
18.8 km

AT THE RECEPTION DESK, the clerk was as unimpressed with my pilgrim effervescence as his predecessor was the night before. I returned my keys and stepped into a black morning, still an hour before sunrise. I trotted down ancient steps leading to the cathedral.

Alone, I crossed the square and disappeared into a narrow street on the opposite side. Fog streamed through town like an Old Testament plague in search of firstborn boys. As the second youngest of eight kids, I'm immune, although I suppose that on this day I could have caught my death of cold. It must have been only a few degrees above freezing – much colder than I had imagined a Spanish spring to be.

Unsure how long it would take to reach the Municipal Pilgrim Office, I hurried so as not to be late for our agreed-upon 7 a.m. rendezvous, in advance of our planned 7:30 departure. I did not want to make Rita and Fujiko wait for me on the inaugural day of our pilgrimage. I arrived at 6:58, feeling smug, if not a little bit anal.

In the communal eat-in kitchen, I found Rita and Fujiko enthusiastically extracting plain yogurt from plastic pouches with their sporks.* They were novitiates, still enjoying the buzz of their recent conversion. More weathered pilgrims – those that might well have started their Camino in Saint-Jean-Pied-de-Port and so had already walked an unbelievable 293.3 km – milled about as though their faith was wearing thin. Listlessly, they squeezed paste out of tubes onto dry toast.

By 7:30, I was champing at the bit, ready to go, for no other reason than that 7:30 had been the time we had said we would leave. One of my biggest hesitations about agreeing to walk the Camino with Fujiko and Rita had been the fear that I would routinely have to wait for them and follow their schedules. I could handle walking 505.2 km, and worried little about scaling the two mountain ranges between this point and Santiago. But having to wait for others was a completely different story.

At 7:33, Rita had disappeared into the loo, blissfully unaware of delaying our 7:30 departure and adding minutes to the day's walk at the wrong end. Rita has always lacked the virtue of temporal obsessiveness on an anal scale, something I know all too well. She is more the type who stands her ground and takes care of herself. And that, it seemed, was what she was doing then, as I twiddled my fingers as calmly as I could.

"Sorry guys, I am going to need a couple more minutes," said Rita, exiting the communal loo on her way to the communal bedroom. I smiled a razor-thin smile and obsessed on how not to obsess so I could just relax and enjoy our first day. Fujiko, our most experienced hiker, was out by the picnic table stretching in the rain. And then, Rita, exactly nine minutes late, was ready to go.

We joined Fujiko and set out on this miserable day I would later describe to friends as idyllic.

----
* A spork is a combination of spoon, fork and knife for scooping, stabbing and slicing at the same time. Invented circa 1874.

Our first task as pilgrims was to find a scallop shell. Any scallop shell. Because the Camino de Santiago de Compostela is lined with them, and they lead the way to the finish line, the great Santiago Cathedral, the eternal resting place of St. James.

We didn't follow real scallop shells, but a variety of facsimiles. They were found on ceramic tiles, inserted in cobblestone walkways or stuck on homes. They were carved in cement on sidewalks and painted on buildings. They could be spotted on bus-stop-like signs standing beside country roads, or etched in manholes, cement posts, lampposts, picnic tables and park benches.

Each graven image signals to pilgrims that they are on the straight and narrow. At various places in the network of small towns across northern Spain, the scallop shells have been replaced by painted arrows. These arrows point this way or that, as if to say, "Move along now, pilgrim." The traditional colour for both scallop shells and arrows is yellow, for reasons that lie beyond my grasp.

"Here's one," said Rita, having spotted a scallop shell about 10 metres ahead. A chill ran down my spine as our official trek to Santiago was set in motion.

For some time, every 10 metres or so there was another shell sighting and one of us would shout, "Here's one!" Then we continued, reassured to know we were still on the right path. Twenty minutes of this and the fact that we had started late vanished from my consciousness, as my age-old obsession with timeliness was replaced with a new one for spotting seashells. I heard a tiny voice in the executive part of my brain telling me what a mess I would be after 25 days of this.

AT 8:17, WE ARRIVED at a major intersection and I was faced with the first great ethical dilemma of the pilgrimage: Would I or would I not obey traffic signals along the way?

The better part of me said I would. The rest of me said that I'm an adult and that I was to use my own judgment: when there is little or no traffic, cross against the lights; otherwise honour and obey.

Most of me (about 84%) thought it was a cut and dried rule. But the other 16% of me wouldn't let me forget that only one day earlier I had signed an oath swearing to be a good pilgrim. If only I had read the oath before signing it, I would have known if it contained a clause about crossing on a red.

Asking ethical questions has a way of leading to more ethical questions, which is why most people prefer not to ask them in the first place. Many prefer to live their lives by adhering to a set of rules without question. It's easier than asking questions, like whether you're the kind of person who would always come to a complete stop at a stop sign even when nobody's around.

Life hums along sweetly when you follow rules without question, until, that is, you wake up one day and realize that following rules, without question, is a questionable practice, which just leads to having to ask questions anyway.

Let's say, for argument's sake, that I choose not to obey traffic signals, I posited to myself, still waiting for the light to change.

Will Spanish children go hungry?

Will Spanish wives let their husband's socks pile up on his side of the bed?

Will Spanish husbands hang out more than they already do at local bars with their buddies?

My answers to these questions were a resounding No, No, and Maybe.

"On the other hand," I asked myself, pushing the button one more time for good measure, "Let's say I will obey traffic signals. What if there is no intersection and, *ipso facto*, no traffic signals either? What will I obey then?"

Maybe Rainer Maria Rilke was right when he said that you must live the questions now and perhaps then, someday far in the future, you will gradually, without even noticing it, live your way into the answer.

Maybe some questions don't have answers until you cross that road.

After an indeterminate amount of time in the rain, I noticed Rita and Fujiko standing safely across the street and staring back at me. The little green man on the traffic light transmuted back into the red man standing still with his hands on hips, forbidding me to proceed.

I made a conscious, albeit split-second decision to disobey and run for it across four lanes of rush-hour traffic.

Cars honked and brakes squealed as the commuting Spanish working class shouted phrases not found in *Collins Spanish Phrase Book & Dictionary*. Sadly, I had no polite response and thus wasted an opportunity to commune with the locals.

"What were you thinking?" demanded Rita, when I got to the other side.

"Please, too many questions," I answered.

"*Mite, mite!*" ("Look, look!") interrupted Fujiko, pointing to another shell, marking the way to where St. James lay waiting with eternal patience for our special visit.

As we were ushered along the northernmost edge of suburban Burgos, through a residential development-in-the-making and past a tiny playground where we stopped for our first break, the shells became infrequent. As we stepped onto a wet path leading across a field and up a ridge to the highway, arrows replaced shells and became even more infrequent still.

I have never been much for noticing important details, so it was a little daunting to realize that I was going to need the observational acuity of an auditor not to wind up in sunny Barcelona rather than the rainier side of Spain, where we were headed. I certainly was not finding the day's pelting rain a motivational force for inching my way closer to Santiago. I don't take an hour to go to church on Sundays, so what in God's name was I thinking when I decided to walk for 25 days to go to one?

The last 5 km were the worst (and longest) and when we finally did arrive at our *albergue*,* marking the end of Day 1, it felt like we had walked a full 24 hours. I was exhausted, and my right knee would no longer bend. When the man running the albergue led us down a flight of stairs to register, I hopped

---

* *Al•ber•gue* (noun): Taken loosely from the the Spanish word "*albergar*," which means to house or accommodate. In English, the word would be hostel, refuge or shelter. *Albergue* is more highfalutin, and so I use it most often.

along behind him like a human pogo stick. To my credit, I hid my pain behind a feeble smile. The gift of suffering, I was repeatedly telling myself, is something many pilgrims would die for. I should try, I thought, to be more grateful.

IT WAS JUST AFTER 10 P.M. and time for my first sleep in a room full of strangers. I was standing, exhausted, next to Bunk No. 16, and every muscle in my body ached. My bed, like all of the others, was made of thin metal tubing. Each had a threadbare mattress, as thick as three slices of cheese. Sleeping in close quarters was not new to me – as a boy, I had camped across Europe with my family of 10 – but it had been decades since I had to do so. And sleeping with strangers is not the same as doubling up with those you love.

Standing next to the bed, I was trying to see how I could vault myself onto the upper bunk without doing myself any harm, or waking Dolores from Hamburg, who was in the bed below. Behind me, a Korean man was having a bad dream. A bald Spanish businessman was on his cell phone and an Irishman was snoring like a lady.

I spread my sleeping bag out flat and quietly unzipped the zipper so as to be able to better slide myself into its pea-pod-like casing. I tried to sense the amount of spring needed to land squarely but softly on top. I rehearsed mentally where I was to place my hands, and how I would hold on so as to cause as little disturbance as possible. Then, I imagined the twist needed to cantilever my body onto the bed. Thankfully, I practise yoga almost religiously, so I was no novice to pretzelling myself in unconventional ways.

With a single vault, I landed on top of the bed as it swayed and squealed its rusty protestations. I lay stock still until the creaking stopped, listening for Dolores from Hamburg's heavy breathing from the bunk below to confirm she was still asleep. Dolores began to grind her teeth and then rolled over. I lay on my back until I was clear what needed to happen next, and then arched myself up ever so slowly until my pelvis was nearly kissing the ceiling and I was supported solely by my shoulders and feet. I poked about with my feet like a hermit crab trying to climb back in its shell. My left foot caught the edge of the sleeping bag but the right slipped off the edge of the bed and I slid back to the floor where I had started. The bed shook but Dolores didn't wake up.

Rita giggled, while Fujiko howled.

«¡*Silencio!*» hissed the bald businessman on his cell phone.

After a few moments to recover, I repeated the process from the beginning. This time, when I arched my pelvis to the ceiling, I held tightly with both hands on opposite sides of the bed. My knuckles turned so white that they could be seen in the dark. I inserted myself into the sleeping bag as if I was squeezing anchovy paste back into the tube.* The ancient springs groaned and moaned as if good times were happening in Bunk No. 16, which was not the case.

I did it! I thought to myself just before Dolores kicked my lower back through the mattress.

"Stop jumping," she snapped.

«¡*Silencio!*» barked the businessman on the cell phone, and the Irishman continued to snore like a lady.

The rest of the night was pretty uneventful. Not much happened, including sleep. The Korean had another nightmare. The businessman eventually put away his cell phone. Someone's intermittent flatulence carried with it the proof of the existence of anchovy paste on toast for dinner. And the Irishman, well, he snored straight through until the first cock crowed before five and the first pilgrims hit the road.

----

* Pilgrims actually eat anchovy paste, and if you walk the Camino, you will too.

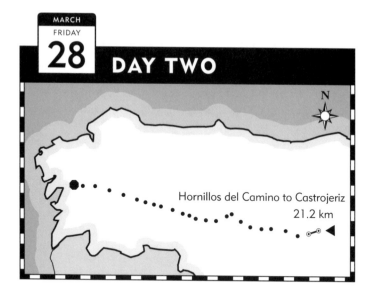

Hornillos del Camino to Castrojeriz
21.2 km

AT 7:04 A.M., I hopped out of bed and said good morning to everyone who kept me up all night. My right knee was not bothering me, except intermittently when it would suddenly give out.

It was my lower back, it seemed, that was going to be my biggest problem. The thin mattress from the night before was so soft that my back was really complaining – and Dolores's jab didn't help either. I did a few yoga stretches and, while I felt better for having done something about it, my back felt worse.

Downstairs in the communal kitchen, pilgrims were tripping over each other as they prepared their breakfasts. At one end of a long wooden table, Rita and Fujiko were busy befriending strangers. At the other end of the long wooden table, I was busy checking my watch.

Not one for small talk, I was anxious to get on the road. But after several seemingly endless minutes, I decided I might as well try to make conversation myself.

"Why are you walking the Camino?" I asked Catherine, a soft-spoken Irish woman opposite me.

Catherine looked at me but said nothing.

"Sorry, is that too personal?" I asked.

Again, Catherine looked at me without a word.

Awkward.

"I didn't mean to offend you," I said. "It's only my second day on the Camino, and I'm not quite up on pilgrim protocol."

"That's okay," said Catherine, softening a little. "People generally don't ask why."

"Why not?"

"People have very personal reasons for walking the Camino."

"Not me," I said. "I'm here because my friends asked me. They caught me in a moment of weakness. And once I said yes, I couldn't say no."

"So you really don't want to be here?"

"Not really."

"So why *are* you?"

"Because I can't say no."

"There must be another reason."

I left the breakfast table not sure what pilgrims talk about. It seemed a little strange to me, coming to do something so obviously communal but then keeping it all to yourself. I mean, 18 of us, most of us strangers, had just spent the night together in the same room. Shouldn't we have had something to talk about over breakfast?

When I arrived upstairs, Rita and Fujiko were waiting by the front door with their packs, ready to go. After a quick pit stop, I joined them with mine and we stepped onto the windy streets of Hornillos del Camino on this cool grey morning.

As we headed out of town, I made a point of waving cheerily and saying *Hola* to the locals who waved back, wishing me a *Buen Camino* as friendly as if I might have been the Pope out of uniform.

The call and response of *Hola*s and *Buen Camino*s was soon replaced with the *Fyu fyu fi fi chi chi chi chika chika chika* of country songbirds. Their calls were the only features in the morning's greenish moonscape. We walked along a treeless valley following the Camino, which disappeared ahead, looking like a ribbon of dirt headed for nowhere. From time to time, a town appeared in the distance but, as we approached, it turned out to be just another pile of rocks.

By 9:40, we climbed out of this featureless valley and stepped onto a vast plain of many fields of green. It looked like a monochromatic quilt stitched together by someone who eats too much granola. Far ahead, there was a strand of sleek white wind turbines. And beyond that was another sea of green.

As we walked through the monotony, my mind began to wander until it fixated on my lower back, which was aching terribly.

"My pack is way too heavy," I complained.

And yet, I knew that I had kept it as light as possible, carefully weighing everything back home. I even included a checklist* in my notebook, because the best guidebooks recommended carrying no more than 10% of your body weight. And therein, I figured, lay the problem.

"The problem is me! I'm too light for my backpack," I said out loud.

So, I sat by the edge of the road and ate as much as I could of the granola I had bought the day before. When I walked on I felt bloated, which convinced me that I got the ratio right. Whenever my back began to hurt, I stopped and ate some more.

TWO HOURS LATER, the plain gave way, leading down to a wide valley. As we approached the edge, the steeple of a church gradually rose before us like the ears of a jackrabbit crouching in the underbrush. It stood in the centre of a picturesque village that lay under the grade of the Meseta, the massive plain that makes up much of Spain's interior. As we approached, I saw a woman sweeping the steps. The tips of her straw broom were white with bird poop from the steps she swept.

«*¿Puedemos* enter *el iglesia?*» I asked, but she immediately put down the broom and walked away.

"What did you say?" asked Rita.

----

* See Appendices A/B for checklists of what to bring/not bring.

"I hope I asked if we could see the church."

Moments later she returned with a giant-sized key and opened the front door. Wordlessly, the three of us stepped into the simple, unadorned, whitewashed space of the 14th century Church of the Assumption.

It had been years since I stepped into a Catholic church other than for family funerals, and I felt a certain sadness. It was a lovely space with simple white walls and light pouring in from square windows just below the ceiling. It made me wonder why I stopped going to church. And that brought back memories of my earliest attempts at understanding the difference between religion, which felt like make-believe, and my own childhood sense of reality, which seemed more matter of fact.

It was Christmas Eve and my large family was crowding around the tree to read the Bible and sing Christmas carols. Our own DIY religious celebration always seemed to coincide with the animated Disney special on TV, which we would be asked to turn off. In my heart of hearts I preferred Disney over religion but I knew I had to pretend it was otherwise. And I knew that Jesus was real while Donald Duck was made up, even though the latter was in Technicolor and so much more fun. Donald Duck always made me feel happy but he was make-believe, whereas Jesus left me feeling empty, yet He was said to be real.

Religion was a bitter medicine that I was given for my own good, I figured. It was an adult reality I entered into every Sunday when the family piled into our VW van to fill a pew at church. As a kid I hoped for the day when I'd see the *Disneyfication* of my beliefs – when my beliefs would be congruent with the wonderful world around me. I longed to swap religious reality with a make-believe that felt true.

Fujiko began to sing a Buddhist chant, its reverberations echoing off the tall white walls and filling the chapel with new life. Rita and I stood in wonder, surrounded by the incomprehensible sounds of her Japanese sutra. When she stopped, we waited in silence for several moments and then turned to leave. At the back of the church, I dropped a few coins in the donation box to quell any guilt that I might have felt for having enjoyed a church experience for free. The old woman nodded and smiled. We did the same and then stepped wordlessly back into daylight.

The Camino descended gently to the bottom of the valley, crossed a river, turned left and continued treeless to the horizon. Fujiko and I talked about Amiko's last days before she died of cancer, stopping occasionally so Rita could apply bandages to the blisters that were forming on her toes and heels. In between stops, I learned that morphine helped control Amiko's suffering in the end. And I heard how she was surrounded by family and one particular friend when she passed on. Amazingly, the friend in question had sent her a card every single day throughout her entire illness. It was a sad story, but I welcomed it as it helped me accept the reality of my friend's passing and to say goodbye.

At around 2 p.m., across the tabletop-like plains, we spotted the remains of Castrojeriz's castle cresting a hill. "A fairytale castle whose make-believe days are over," I sighed to myself.

WE ATE LUNCH on the patio of *La Puerta del Monte* Hotel (☆☆).* The owner, Renaldo, escorted us to a table in a sunny corner of the restaurant's terrace that offered a view of a church below and the ruined castle above. After lunch, we decided to check into the hotel and paid in advance. We then headed up the grand double staircase and dispersed into our rooms to shower and wash our clothes.

Around 7 p.m., Renaldo and his wife Pabla knocked on my door to let me know that they were leaving for the night.

"Make yourself at home," they said, and then disappeared. I guess we have the place to ourselves, I thought to myself.

Moments later, there was a knock on the door and Renaldo and Pabla reappeared.

---

* The hotel star system at times can feel like reading tea leaves: how can you really be sure you are interpreting them correctly? One day a two-star hotel might turn out to be a hole, and the next a little piece of heaven. *La Puerta del Monte* Hotel was a piece of heaven (with mattresses as soft as clouds, but not in a good way).

"I forget," said Renaldo. "Tonight, there is a small *fiesta de bautismo* in the hotel."

"A baptismal party?" I confirmed.

«*Si*», he answered.

"They will be peaceful," assured Pabla.

A lot of things can be said to describe the baptismal party that began around 10 p.m. and broke up just before dawn, but "peaceful" is not one of them. Unless by "peaceful," Pabla meant that they would be too busy dancing to start a revolution.

Lying in bed listening to them carry on, I couldn't help but think how staid my own religious upbringing was in comparison. We'd self-consciously sing carols around the Christmas tree and then scurry to bed, whereas the Spanish, from cradle to grave, whoop it up all night long.

Unfortunately, I was way too tired to get out of bed and join in, so I just laid awake listening to their laughter, feeling like the outsider that I was. The more the Spanish people partied, the more reserved and Canadian I felt. I tried to quiet them with a passive-aggressive fantasy in which I encouraged them to swing at a *piñata* that was really a hornet's nest I had painted yellow, but it only backfired because my imagination gone wild just kept me awake as well. After they finished, around 5 a.m., I finally drifted off to sleep.

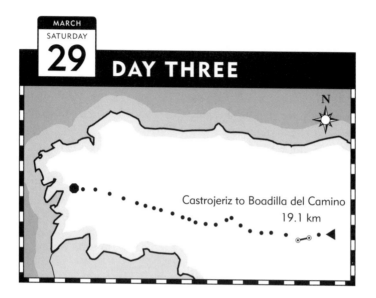

Castrojeriz to Boadilla del Camino
19.1 km

RENALDO AND PABLA hadn't arrived back at the hotel, so we left our keys behind the front desk and let ourselves out. We passed through the hotel's large metal gate and found ourselves back on the Camino for another day. The street was deserted except for a little black dog that bounced up and down, cartoon-like, on all four feet when it saw us. Overhead, the sky was bluish and the sun promised warmth, if it could only burn away the mist. As we took the main road through town, followed by the little black dog bouncing along behind us, Fujiko sang the Japanese version of *Kindred Spirits*. Then, as we arrived at a corner where three banks were crowding the local police station, Fujiko stopped suddenly.

"What's wrong, Fujiko?" asked Rita.

"*Boshi wo wasuremashita.* I forget hat!" said Fujiko.

"Uh-oh. Did you lock the gate?" I asked.

"Never lock gate," said Fujiko. "Bad luck."

As Fujiko retreated up the lane to the hotel, Rita and I waited in silence. We were just three days into the walk and I had ostensibly mastered the art of waiting for others. My need to depart on time had vanished and, in its place, was a certain

23

fascination with counting the minutes between when we said we would leave and when we actually did. A lot can get done in 12.5 otherwise wasted minutes waiting for others. For one thing, it's an excellent time to think. And that made me glad because, from what I understood, thinking is one of the things pilgrims are supposed to do a lot of on the Camino. And unless I've got it wrong, it all starts with wondering what I'm supposed to be thinking about.

Let me see, I thought to myself, should I think about the money I'm not earning by not speaking at the engagements I turned down to be here? Should I fixate on how it wasn't my idea to walk in the rainy season? Or should I just meditate on my guilt for having these thoughts in the first place, rather than being a better person?

Fujiko returned wearing her hat, looking like she was part of the Asian tour of *Anne of Green Gables*.

"It was by the door," said Fujiko laughing.

I couldn't see what was funny about finding a hat by a door but the women kept laughing and I eventually joined in. We laughed all the way down the hill to the edge of town at absolutely nothing at all, and I completely forgot my funk. At the bottom, the fog was so thick we could barely see across a roundabout. That put an end to our laughing.

Rita pulled out her guidebook and looked out over a traffic circle the way Moses might have looked over the Red Sea. Meanwhile, Fujiko flagged down a tiny little Spanish car to ask for directions. The driver was either showing no pity at all or was so squished he couldn't lift his foot off the gas pedal to press the brakes. In any case, he swerved around us, and sped up the hill into town. Fujiko flagged down another car, which slowed but didn't actually stop.

«¿*Cual* road is for *el Camino*?» I asked, walking alongside the car.

«*La primera a la derecha*», ("the first on the right") said the driver before she sped up the hill and into town, too.

"Jeez, for a small town, people sure are in a hurry," said Rita.

Sure enough, the first road on the right was the way to Santiago, as evidenced by a scallop shell barely visible in the mist. We crossed the traffic circle and began what would be a 19.1-km walk, give or take a few hundred metres for sightseeing and/or finding lunch.

Where the fog was thinnest, the sun shone through and the landscape appeared colourized, like an old tinted photo. Up ahead, beyond the mist, there appeared to be a hill. That would be the day's expected 100-metre vertical climb. We ascended along a single-lane dirt road as it bent left then right around the side of the barren hill, with the odd aubergine-coloured bush appearing from time to time.

I was wearing what I like to call my mountain flip-flops. They are hiking boots with heels that have separated at the back, so they flip-flopped like beach sandals when I walked. I had worn them to the top of Mount Fuji, Japan's highest mountain, and back again, and I felt loyal to them. Although they were almost ready to meet their maker, I refused to let them go. They still offered good ankle support while being so light that I hardly knew I had them on. And, perhaps most importantly, they had never given me blisters. I didn't care if the Camino was lined with far better hiking boots tossed aside by pilgrims who'd moved on; I intended to wear my mountain flip-flops until I gave up the ghost or they gave up their soles.

Step by step, we climbed the hill until we eventually escaped the fog into the soothing warmth of the direct sun. Silhouetted in the distance, black on white, was yesterday's castle, floating fairytale-like on a cloud as it was meant to do.

At the very top, we stopped for breakfast at cement picnic tables placed thoughtfully so that pilgrims could enjoy the view, and I ate as much of the remaining granola as I could. Throughout breakfast, the sun burned away the clouds that were masking the plain below. As it did, it robbed the castle above Castrojeriz of its cottony perch, exposing rooftops lower down. Once breakfast was over, we gathered our garbage, mindful to carry out what we carried in, and continued west on a flat plain for about 1 km. After "oohing" and "aahing" over another exquisite view, we descended a steep stony road in one straight unrelenting line, as if we were tracing a giant yellow arrow to the bottom.

It was a struggle to descend slowly and my right knee seized up painfully every fourth or fifth step before giving way.

At the end of the steady decline, we stepped into a long valley, where I soon saw *www.bahai.org* spray-painted in black on an official Camino sign. The followers of the Bahá'í faith were not the only ones defacing or misusing the sacred iconography of the Camino. In three short days, I had noticed that the scallop shells and yellow arrows intended to keep pilgrims on the path were used almost as much to lead them off. Restaurants, hotels and shops, anywhere from 50–1,500 metres off the Camino, tried to lure us away with arrows, promising anything from authentic Spanish omelette to private rooms with baths and rain ponchos.

To hungry and weather-worn pilgrims, these distractions could be as seductive as candy to children, light bulbs to moths, equations to scientists or typos to proofraeders,* so we had to be careful when straying from the official route. Whether or not you could actually find these businesses or whether they were open when you got there was another story. I resisted the urge to follow a tiny dirt road to visit a private museum, choosing to head straight for Boadilla del Camino and a guaranteed lunch, dinner and bed, instead.

For the rest of the morning we walked through rich green fields of buckwheat, which looked like rocky golf courses gone fallow. We traveled from one long valley to another, each a world of its own, with its own geography, feel and character. There were no peaks in this land of high plains and deep valleys. Some might say that when God sculpted it, He ran out of plasticine to make the mountaintops.

We inched past a poplar grove that was planted in such complete geometric perfection that the deer wandering through it must have thought God was a retired accountant with a hobby farm. Then we crossed a narrow stone bridge where traffic could go east or west at any moment, but never both at the same time. On the western side, we stepped off the bridge into the province of Palencia demarcated with an

---

* Misspelled on purpose, hopefully with comic effect.

official sign (with *www.bahai.org* spray-painted in black in the lower right-hand corner). We followed the road to the left, and turned our backs on the wind turbines that had escorted us to the edge of their territory.

TIRED AND WEARY, we arrived mid-afternoon in the sleepy town of Boadilla del Camino. Boadilla del Camino looked like the set of *Gunsmoke*, two years after its final season. We followed handwritten signs to *En el Camino*, which soon led us off the trail, down dusty roads to a final cardboard sign that was covered in a protective sheet of weathered plastic. The sign was affixed to a stucco wall that might have once been painted a sprightly pink. It hung on a decaying string around a rusty spike. Beside the sign, a decrepit barn-wood door served as the humble entrance to *En el Camino*, where we hoped to find private rooms for the night.

"Doesn't look like much," said Rita.

"It reminds me of the peasant homes in the Romanian village where my grandparents were born," I added.

Rita took the lead, as she would throughout much of the Camino, and pushed the wooden door open. It fell off its hinges onto the dirt with a thud. Then we stepped into an unlit, untended barn of a space. On our left, there was a dorm-style room with perhaps 26 beds. Straight ahead, though, we found an immaculately tended inner courtyard of green grass, colourful gardens and steel sculptures. There, pilgrims who passed us on the road were relaxing in the garden, chatting in twos and threes, like members of a strange cult promising salvation to those who walk at least 20 km a day. A freshly finished sidewalk led to the modern facade of a home up ahead. A quiet and friendly curly-haired man in his late twenties stepped out of the house, followed by two mutts.

"Welcome," he said, arms outstretched. "My name is Jesus."*

"Really?" I said, before I could catch myself.

----

* In Spanish the name is actually Jesús and is pronounced "Hey, Zeus!", but it's the same name. It's simpler to just think Jesus, the way we say it.

I'd heard that a lot of people in Latin countries are named Jesus, but this was the closest I had ever been to a real live One.

As Jesus shook our hands, his dogs threatened to lick us into oblivion.

The atmosphere at *En el Camino* was so relaxed it felt as if it would be an offence to even suggest we might be there on business, such as, for example, to rent three private rooms.

After a full 10 minutes to chill (that nearly killed me), interspersed by the odd nicety (that prolonged my agony), I couldn't take any more.

"We're hoping for private rooms. Do you have any?" I smiled stiffly to show that I meant no harm.

"Sure. We have three," said Jesus. He signed us in and said we could pay "whenever".

Leading us up a grand wooden staircase to the *first* floor (which back home would be considered the *second**), Jesus showed us to our private rooms, which faced each other across the empty space carved out by the stairs. My room, with two single beds, a wooden chair and an armoire, was simple. However, it had a wall of windows that opened to the happy sounds of pilgrims in the sunny garden below. Rita's opened to the sleepy town and Fujiko's stared at a wall, but they were both happy campers not to be sleeping in the dormitory with the rabble.

Satisfied that we were content with our rooms, Jesus led us downstairs and introduced us to his mother, Sabina, a kind middle-aged woman who I could see had given him his curly hair. Smiling, Sabina wiped her hands on her white apron and shook each of ours. She led us into a wood-panelled dining room and seated us at the end of a long table, closest to the window. Jesus returned to tell us what his mother had made for us that day and began to serve a fabulous home-cooked meal.

After lunch, we dispersed and spent the afternoon sleeping off our morning walk, washing clothes and hanging them off radiators and doorknobs, and chatting with other pilgrims in the yard.

----

* In Spain, you will find the *first* floor on the *second*, the *second* on the *third*, the *third* on the *fourth*, and so on.

FUJIKO AND RITA went to bed early that evening, too tired to eat, and so I dined alone. Alone at my end of the table that is. At the opposite end of the table, a heavyset German man talked to Dolores from Hamburg – who I decided to forgive for having jabbed me in the back two nights earlier – and her husband, Helmut. I resented feeling obligated to join their conversation, as I would rather have kept company with my own thoughts. But I joined in anyway, and soon learned all about a miraculous green paste that Dolores was rubbing into her husband's stiff muscles at the end of every day.

After Dolores and Helmut left, the German man sat in silence for a few moments and then lifted himself out of his chair and sat himself next to me. I was just starting my second course, a large plate of long thin green beans when he unburdened himself of his story.

"My *vife* is a shaman *oont* I am too," he said. "*Vee* learned every*ss*ing from *zee* Inuit in *Kanada*."

"Really?" I asked, glancing at my beans.

"I speak *viss* angels," he added.

I sucked a bean into my mouth. As I poked another one with my fork, he leaned forward and stared intensely into my eyes.

"*Ziss* room is *f-f-f-full* of angels," he announced. "*Zey* are standing all *r-r-r-round* me."

In my world, the dining room was empty but, in his, it was standing room only.

"Some people need facts: I don't," he added.

Me neither. I don't believe in facts, I thought to myself wryly.

After another excruciatingly long pause, he leaned even closer. Our faces were so close that an angel at the far end of the room would swear we were star-crossed lovers. Eating another bean before he disengaged seemed ill-advised. I just couldn't be sure there was enough space to do so without it seeming like I was inviting him to nibble on one end while I nibbled on the other. He looked deeply into my eyes looking for – I don't know – a light shining out the other end?

"Have you felt pain on *ziss* tr-r-r-rip?" asked the shaman, suddenly doubling as a kind of family doctor that makes uninvited house calls.

"My right knee has been bothering me."

"It *vill* come again *oont* it *vill* get *vorse*," said the healer.

Then he cocked his head to one side with an otherworldly expression.

As Jesus returned to swap my empty plate for a bowl of strawberries and cream, I wanted to shout, *«¡Salva me Jesús!»* But he vanished as quickly as he appeared.

On the outside, I ate the berries and cream and smiled at the shaman between bites. But on the inside, I was pissed, and the angels must have known it. What right had this man to ask me if I was feeling any pain and then tell me it was going to get worse? It struck me as infinitely irritating psychobabble. Ask 99.999% of all pilgrims if they had felt pain, and with the exception of those who were currently high on Spanish omelette, the answer would be a resounding "yes". You don't have to row a boat to the far reaches of Baffin Island and then pilfer an ancient belief system to know that. This wasn't communing with angels; it was *The Human Condition 101*.

Not only that, but follow up that question by telling 99.999% of all pilgrims that the pain is going to get worse and you are going to scare the bejesus out of them. Try this on a pilgrim whose right knee has been seizing up since the first day of a 505.2-km walk, and you're going to freak him out. Why? Because he had only slept 12 hours in three days, and he was tired and sore. On top of *that*, everything about this country was particularly Spanish in ways that he was not. On top of that, at the very core of his being, he was wrestling with why he ever agreed to go on this infernal expedition in the first place. Wouldn't he rather be living his passion, which is performing funny talks at conventions back home (not to mention putting food on the table as he does it)?

"You know *ziss* pain," added the great kahuna. "You know *vat* it is about. But it is not about *vat* you are carrying; it is about *how* you are carrying it. Change how you carry it and it *vill* go away."

He paused as if he might be wondering if I was saving the last strawberry for him.

As I put it in my mouth he added the final whammy, "It is something that has been *t-r-r-r-roubling* you for years."

That said, he looked at me and I looked at him. Then he got up and bid me a *"Gute Nacht"*, with the full weight of a German medicine man who owed it all to the aboriginal people of Canada.

A few minutes later, I headed back to my room, wishing Jesus a good night before climbing the stairs to bed. I closed the door to my room behind me and stood in the dark. Too tired to head down the hall to brush my teeth, I slipped into the single bed closest to the window.

What if Mr. Know-It-All was right? I wondered, my heart beating too fast to fall asleep. What if my knee gave out the next day, or the day after, or halfway up a mountain?

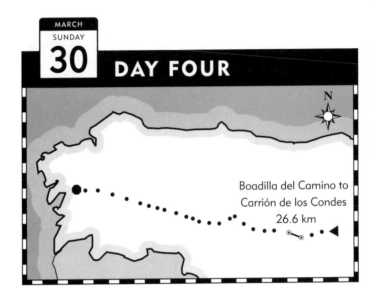

Boadilla del Camino to
Carrión de los Condes
26.6 km

WHEN I GOT UP THAT MORNING, I could feel that the constant walking was slowly catching up with me. Frankly, I felt more tired than when I went to sleep. I crawled out of bed and tested to see if my right knee was working. It was.

Maybe I changed how I am carrying it *al-r-r-r-ready*, I thought to myself.

It was the fourth day of walking and, on top of the fatigue, I had noticed that I was starting to feel guilty too. I was feeling guilty for not being as religious or pensive as I could have been. But then, was it just me? Or was it hard to contemplate everlasting peace when Noah's flood was about to break? I'm no weatherman but the sky looked as though it could burst at any moment, and we had 26.6 km ahead of us.

After breakfast, we headed out of town on a well-marked path that led us to an octopus of on-and-off-ramps at Highway N-611. Once at the top, though, there was a sea of construction, where signs directed the cars down exit ramps and whisked them off to alternate routes and secondary roads. We pilgrims, on the other hand, were left to fend for ourselves through the muck.

In North America, construction sites are strictly off-limits to accident-prone mortals like us. They are considered dangerous, an invitation to return to God early, leaving relatives to sue for damages once the victim's remains have been recovered. Not so in Spain. We were free to roam through the goo, play in puddles and even climb on bulldozers.

The muddy scene took me back to when my little sister and I used to play in the farmers' fields after the heavy rains in May delayed the planting of soybeans. We would put on our older siblings' black rubber boots, which reached up to our knees. This was good because that's about how deep we hoped to sink when we reached the far corner of the field where it was wettest. We always brought along our neighbour Suzie from across the street because we could count on her to get fabulously stuck in the mud.

My sister and I were in search of quicksand and Suzie was brought along in case we were lucky enough to find some. I'll never forget the day we did. Suzie sank instantly to her knees and then, ever so slowly, she tipped over backward until she was lying on her back, where she cried for us to save her. We did, of course, but only after pretending to leave her there and almost getting stuck ourselves.

When we dropped Suzie off, her mother got so mad that all she could say was, "You children!"* Back at our own house, we washed ourselves off with the hose and then snuck in front of the TV set with the rest of our siblings, our earlier absence unnoticed by our parents.

Remembering all this, it was hard to resist the urge to stay and play all day in the construction site. As an adult, it doesn't matter how dirty I get: there is nobody to upset. This would have been more fun than walking. Yet Rita was on the move, so five metres into the construction area, our shoes caked thick with muck, I resisted the urge to dally and obediently followed.

In the distance, a dotted line of hunchbacked pilgrims stretched into the grey horizon through the fog. Strung along

----

* Mothers in my neighbourhood had anger issues in the '70s; they couldn't express it very well, poor dears.

behind them, we spotted scallop shells carved into cement pylons, which confirmed that we were still headed for Santiago.

AS A FIERCE STORM came in from the west, the next 10 km proved to be so miserable they would have ended marriages. The skinniest would have been blown away, while the fattest would have sunk into the mud: neither ever to be seen at the buffet of life again. The oldest and youngest wouldn't have made it either. During the initial squall, we secured waterproof covers over each other's backpacks and fastened them tightly with string. While we were at it, we battened down our rain ponchos until we looked like Mother Nature's prisoners, which we were. To her credit though, she delivered us wiser if not wearier than when we had set out.

I for one had my eyes opened to an important, albeit painful, fact: my trusted water-resistant walking pants were not the pants I thought they were. In fact, they were the clothing equivalent of passive aggressive. They seemed as if they would keep me dry, but the moment they could, they betrayed me, letting the rain pass through to soak and chill me to the bone.

We found only three refuges that afternoon. The first was a hovel of a bar found through a hole in a hedge. When we arrived, the rain stopped. Once we were ready to go, it picked up again. The second was the touristy town of Villalcázar de Sirga, where we stopped by the *Santa María la Blanca* Church, which was famous for a kind of medieval peep show of the complete and unadulterated life of St. James. At one euro a pop, the *retablos** lit up so you could see the holy man's life, as clear as day, right up to where he lost his head and wound up in a field to be found later by a shepherd and carried in a modified piggyback fashion to Santiago. After that, we visited a bakery, messily eating sweet after sweet and leaving only when we looked like we had been dipped in icing sugar.

----

* *Re•ta•blos* (noun): Something above and behind an altar like a table or a series of pictures. In this case, it was both a series of pictures *and* a table.

As we walked the last 5.8 km to Carrión de los Condes, I thought about the historic town of Villalcázar de Sirga that we had just visited. In fact, I thought about the history that I had been literally walking through all along the Camino de Santiago de Compostela. It occurred to me that I was not particularly overtaken by it. If I had not been so reluctant to go on this pilgrimage in the first place, I might have read something about it before I had arrived. If only I had, I'd be a veritable know-it-all on all things St. James.

I'd know for example that the word *compostela* isn't the Spanish word for composting garden waste, but is, instead, a lovely, if not overly flowery word meaning "field of stars". It was in such a dimly-lit *compostela* that a particular Spanish shepherd named Pelayo stumbled upon what was left of the martyred St. James (circa 814 A.D.), hence beginning the cult that gave birth to one of the world's most trodden pilgrimages.

Camino de Santiago de Compostela all together means "the way of St. James of the field of stars". It doesn't sound very macho, and yet St. James, by all accounts, was a man's man – rough and tumble and ready for a fight. Why else would Jesus Christ have given James and his brother John the monicker of *Boanerges* (or "Sons of Thunder" for those of us who can't read Aramaic as well as Mel Gibson)?

If only I had done my homework, I'd be up on the Knights Templar as well, the order of knights who built the *Santa María la Blanca* church we'd just visited. According to Rita, they erected the church in the 13th century, along with countless others along the Camino, just as their influence was gaining steam. A major part of their *raison d'être* was to look out for pilgrims like us while making the lives of the poor Moors a living hell. Until, that is, their power and popularity grew to the point that Pope Gregory and King Philip of France, feeling *über*-threatened, finally said "Enough is enough!" and did away with them via the bloody massacre of Jacques de Molay, the Grand Master of the Order, and most of the Knights Templar. For this event, they chose Friday the 13th, October 1307. Friday the 13th has not been the same since.

It's interesting to know about history because what happened then affects what happens now. It explains things, and makes present behaviour, such as superstition around Friday the 13th, less of a mystery. But sometimes it's hard to care about history, especially when our lives get overly busy. On the Camino, it was not as though I had a million things to do, but I was rather preoccupied with doing one thing: putting one foot in front of the other a million times.

Most pilgrims, from what I could see, were like me. They were not as interested in the fact that Prince Felipe, younger brother of Alfonso X, lay in eternal rest at the *Santa María la Blanca* church, as they were in thinking about where the nearest grocery store was, what time they would get to their *albergue*, and how they hoped to get a good night's sleep that night.

WE ARRIVED AT THE FAMOUS Santa Clara Monastery just as our spiked sugar levels from having visited the bakery in historic Villalcázar de Sirga took a dive. Reception was full of boxed cookies and other evidence (but no proof) of the existence of the Sisters of Santa Clara, the nuns who are said to inhabit this place. A tiny man checked us in, and Fujiko bought three boxes of the nuns' cookies, an astounding 897 grams more for her to carry (or a fairly light snack, which we actually devoured minutes later).

The moment we were through checking in, the man nodded and we knew we were supposed to follow him across the compound to a large wooden door leading to the sleeping quarters. After scurrying for our backpacks, we caught up with him in front of the door.

"The key is here always. Behind the shutter. You turn the key to the left. You open the door. You put the key back. You always put the key back. Everybody uses the key. We close at 10. Go inside," said the tiny man running the nunnery.

Rita, Fujiko and I looked at each other.

"Go *inside*!" he repeated, only louder this time.

"Here is the microwave. A table to take your meals. Turn right. Shower. Shower. Shower. Go outside. Here is laundry.

Shower. Shower. Shower. Toilet. Toilet. Toilet. Go inside. Here is your room. Put your things on the bed. To get out, you pull on the door."

And he started to leave.

"Excuse me, I have question," said Fujiko. Rita and I, standing side by side, looked at each other without moving our heads.

The man turned ever so slowly toward Fujiko, stopping halfway, still with his back to us.

"Is there heating?" asked Fujiko.

"I already told you at check-in! Starting at eight o'clock," said the man, heading out again.

"Is Mass tonight?" asked Fujiko. Rita and I looked at each other again. Fujiko was on a roll. A very dangerous roll.

"No," said the man. "Only tomorrow morning at 8:30."

The man stood still for several seconds, then spoke again. "Pilgrims leave by 8 a.m. Thank you."

And he left, as our bedroom door slammed behind him with a metallic clang. Moments later, we heard the heavy wooden door slam too, and we watched him cross the courtyard and disappear into the office.

"Boy, if he's that tough I can hardly wait to see what the nuns are like," said Rita.

Our bedroom featured four metal-framed single beds and a naked bulb hanging from the ceiling. It was what I imagined the Czar and his family would have been offered in Siberia shortly before they met their untimely ends. Each bed had its own *"asiento"*, a kind of interfacing-like fabric that we were to use to cover the mattress and then dispose of in the morning.

AT 10 P.M. SHARP, the tiny man returned to switch off the lights. He did so without comment, and then left, the large wooden door slamming behind him. Through the bars on the bedroom window, we watched his shadow escape through a tiny door in the thick fortress-like gate of the monastery. We could hear him turn a key to lock us in. Staying at the Santa Clara Monastery was like paying €7 for a night at Alcatraz. Technically we were guests but it felt more like being under house arrest. To be fair, Santa Clara did offer the creature comforts we had come to expect on the Camino: a bed, a shower and a toilet, each as communal as it was cold.

DAY FIVE

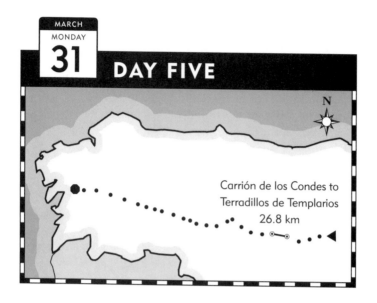

Carrión de los Condes to
Terradillos de Templarios
26.8 km

"TODAY IS GOING TO BE A CAKE WALK," announced Rita. "There are no services between here and Terradillos de Templarios."

Cake walks, we had decided, were any walks without services for more than 15 km, including cake. Not only were they without emergency help should we have, heaven forbid, needed it, but they lacked the dignity of toilets and also required that we carry extra food and water too. None of us had been looking forward to the extra load. And on this day we were walking 26.8 km – our longest day yet.

As the 8 a.m. checkout time approached, we rushed between kitchen, showers, toilets and bedrooms, anxious to get out before the tiny man returned to lock the gate. As I collected my clothes from the cold radiators in the bedroom, they were still wet and I harboured several unkind thoughts toward the nuns. I tied the clothes to my backpack like flags of surrender, hoping they would dry during the day. Fifteen minutes before the ungodly checkout time, we left the Santa Clara Monastery for good.

Or so we thought.

Down the street, we popped into a bar full of Spanish men smoking cigarettes for breakfast. A few were drinking coffee. We ordered genetically modified croissants that were so big they were served on a dinner plate with knife and fork. Then we planned our escape from this reputedly nun-infested town. Rita's scheme included a stop at the bank for cash, the hardware store for phone cards, the pharmacy for bandages and the grocery store for tons of food.

But just as we were about to leave, Fujiko threw her hands up to her mouth, which in Japanese means "I am about to tell you about *another* disaster that could have been avoided."

"My hat! I forget it in man's nunnery," she said.

"Uh-oh, this could get ugly," said Rita.

The large clock above the bar read 8:06, a full six minutes after the tiny man had no doubt locked the gate. We hurried back to the monastery with little hope. Our hope, being little, had been the appropriate size: the gate was indeed locked.

"We go to Mass and pray. Is it a good idea?" said Fujiko. So, at 8:17 we spent several minutes trying to figure out how to get through a complex set of doors and heavy velvet drapes that separated the outside world from the holy sanctuary. Once we managed to navigate this ecclesiastical obstacle course, we entered and witnessed Mass being attended by two local women, the priest and the three of us. I was surprised by how few people were in the church as I noticed a warm Mediterranean breeze blowing through the nave.

"So this is what the nuns are doing with our seven euros," I said. "They're heating their bloody church with it."

Just then, the church filled with the sound of crackly women's voices simmering on low. I turned my neck to see a group of ramshackle nuns dressed head to toe in black. Standing behind an elaborate wrought-iron screen in the dimly lit recesses of the church, the nuns of Santa Clara Monastery were almost impossible to detect.

"Look!" exclaimed Fujiko. Rita stared too, but I couldn't bring myself to look back again after an initial glance.

"I think they might prefer their privacy," I whispered.

"Please," said Rita, under her breath. "I paid seven euros."

Rita and Fujiko seemed quite comfortable gawking at the nuns, but I felt it was rude. Besides, who was left to pay attention to the priest? As a young child, I'd felt it was my job to make the Mass work as much as it was the clergy's. They might have had the most lines, I figured, but unless I showed my respect by sitting up straight and paying attention, none of the magic would rub off on me. And so I was sitting stiffly at this moment, maybe even more politely than the two local women in attendance.

As we reached the part of the service known as the offering, where we're meant to express our gratitude for all that we've been given, a young soprano voice rose over the static of the elderly nuns, and we were led through a call and response. One of the local women stopped by our pew with a basket and I made good on my heartfelt thanks by tossing in some loose change.

For the rest of the Mass I pretended to pay attention, but I was really replaying the shaman's words in my head.

"You know *ziss* pain. You know *vat* it is about..."

How could he have known that I knew, when I was not even sure myself? Or was I just pretending not to know?

At the end of Mass, the priest disappeared into the sacristy and the two local women called out «¡Buen Camino!»

Then we stepped outside and discovered that, against all odds, the monastery's gate was open and the man who ran the nunnery was just about to leave.

«¡Buenos días!» exclaimed Fujiko. "Boshi wo Wasuremashita. I forget my hat!"

«Buen Camino», he said as he turned and smiled the tiniest smile.

Moments later, Fujiko returned, wearing her hat and looking like Anne of Green Gables once again. The man locked the door to the monastery and rode off on his bicycle, but not without turning to wish us «Buen Camino» one last time.

"Our seven euros went pretty far after all," said Rita. "The church was warm, the nuns put on a good show and that little man smiled at us. Everything is as it should be."

And so our cake walk began.

Wanting to record how long a 26.8-km day was, I wrote down key events in my notebook along with specific times.

The 26.8-Km Cake Walk

9:15 a.m.: Errands completed, the cake walk begins.

9:33 a.m.: A giant stone arch at the edge of town marks the end of civilization.

10:15 a.m.: The day is hot and getting hotter.

10:35 a.m.: We crowd a small tree like goats, vying for shade to cool off.

11:08 a.m.: Rita struggles with her load and lists to the right.

11:09 a.m.: I wonder whether to help her or not.

11:10 a.m.: I decide not to, rationalizing that on the Camino, spiritual considerations trump common courtesy; if she is carrying too much, she has to manage it herself.

12:45 p.m.: We stop for lunch in the middle of a field under a high sun.

12:48 p.m.: I discover that my yogurt has turned to feta cheese.

1:05 p.m.: I decide I have almost enough water to survive.

1:33 p.m.: We descend another steep ridge and my knee gives out repeatedly.

1:38 p.m.: I make a mental list of everything I could carry differently from groceries to grudges but nothing seems connected to the pain in my knee.

1:43 p.m.: I remember how my yoga teacher said to pull up on my quadriceps when I walk. When I try it, my knee feels instantly better.

1:55 p.m.: I enjoy feeling superior to the shaman and his meddling crew of know-it-all angels.

2:05 p.m.: I drink the last of my water and wonder if the angels are going to get me back.

3:36 p.m.: We walk into Terradillos de Templarios just before I die of thirst.

3:45 p.m.: Brazilians in a box-like hotel give us private rooms down a deserted hall.

3:53 p.m.: I wash my clothes in the sink with one sachet of shampoo and save a second for me.

3:59 p.m.: In the shower I hop and twist, flashing various parts, long enough to rinse without freezing.

4:18 p.m.: I write the same message in 23 postcards: "Wish you were here ... instead of me."

5:30 p.m.: I check emails on an ancient computer with coin-operated Internet access.

6:49 p.m.: The familiar routine of deleting 858 junk emails makes me feel homesick.

8:30 p.m.: We eat dinner with two Austrian girls who, while they seem fit, are bussing it part way.

8:33 p.m.: They think Rita and I are married but we explain how we're just friends who worked in insurance together.

8:45 p.m.: They tell us their life stories, starting over from the beginning whenever they realize we've stopped listening.

8:55 p.m.: The Austrian girls ask how long Rita and I have been married. Rita holds my hand.

9:01 p.m.: Something doesn't feel right.

9:30 p.m.: I rush to the toilet having caught the plague.

9:35 p.m.: Fujiko brings me Chinese tea and pills and says it's heat stroke.

9:40 p.m.: I am lying on the floor and can't get up.

9:42 p.m.: I ask Rita to perform the last rites.

10:05 p.m.: Back on the toilet. It isn't pretty.

10:15 p.m.: I crawl into bed, shivering. I need sympathy but the women have gone to sleep, so I pity myself. It's like a drug.

10:28 p.m.: I fall asleep.

11:02 p.m.: Back on the toilet for Round 3.

11:08 p.m.: The long crawl back.

11:39 p.m.: I fall asleep – or die. Impossible to tell which.

1 a.m.: I wake up in a cold sweat, unfit to continue. Hallelujah!!! This is my chance to bail.

6 a.m.: I wake up feeling well enough to walk ... Damnation!

Sunny with nauseous periods.

DAY SIX

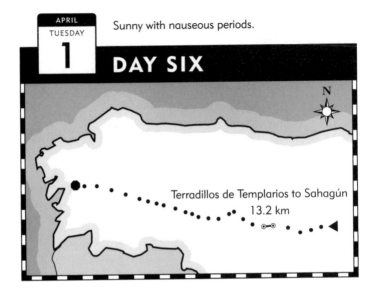

Terradillos de Templarios to Sahagún
13.2 km

WE ARRIVED in San Nicolás del Real Camino for lunch, a town that had its poverty concealed under a generous layer of dust. We stopped at the only restaurant-bar and ordered cheese omelette sandwiches. As an afterthought, Fujiko asked for pickles, which the proprietor dropped on the floor, wiped off and put on a plate before adding them to the bill with a pencil from behind his ear.

We ate outside in the square, sitting on white plastic chairs at a round plastic table. An elderly couple arrived like cross-country skiers in search of winter. They were a sight, with matching ski poles and matching blue plastic cups tied with string to their waists. As they came nearer we recognized them as Dolores, the German woman I saw rub green paste into her husband Helmut's muscles the other night, and the man himself. We learned that they were both 80 years old and were walking about 20 km a day, like us. This was their sixth Camino, and I found it a small miracle that they were still together. Dolores bounced like the little black dog in Castrojeriz. Helmut lumbered like an old dog who'd been led down this road before.

As Dolores and Helmut found a place at the next table, two young men pulled up in the only shiny thing in town, a red convertible. They hopped out of the car and headed for the bar. The owners met them in the doorway, beers in hand as though they were expecting them. There was much kissing of cheeks, laughter, and lively chatter, followed by two more beers washed down with cigarettes. The two men hopped back into the red convertible and sped out of town, continuing on their own adventure.

Our sandwiches arrived, each comprised of a huge fluffy omelette on what seemed like a whole loaf of bread. As we ate, Dolores asked Rita and I how long we had been together. We found ourselves once again explaining that we were not a couple, and threw in that Fujiko was not a hanger-on we met at the airport.

"We climbed Mount Fuji together," explained Rita.

Perhaps re-energized by the thought of Japan's highest mountain, Dolores was suddenly on her feet again and ready to go. Helmut was not quite as keen. He stared into space for a few moments, and then rose slowly. He took two steps after Dolores, turned to us, rolled his eyes and groaned, «Buen Camino».

About a quarter of an hour later, on our own way out of town, I smiled and waved at every local I saw. I felt silly doing it, but the behaviour was completely beyond my control. There was just something about putting on my backpack that made me act like an idiot. And I was not alone. Rita and Fujiko smiled and waved too, as did virtually every other pilgrim on the Camino. You would think we would have wanted to balance how stupid we looked with a more dignified demeanour. Instead, we compulsively behaved as dumb as we appeared. Put a backpack on me and set me in motion and I turn into the ambassador of asininity.

Somewhere between here and Burgos I had decided that movement must have something to do with it. The fact that we wave like idiots when we, or others like us, are in motion is at the very core of our humanity. Passengers on boats, from the smallest of pleasure craft to the largest of cruise ships, wave like morons, as do onlookers standing on shore. People on trains wave reflexively too, as do those who watch them rush by. Nobody is above this. Even royalty, as much as they try to rein it in, will give the most restrained of waves, looking like total fools in their motorcades. And we wave right back, as if we never learned any better.

Frankly, we have nobody to blame but ourselves. What do we do when babes in arms wave like idiots? We encourage them by waving just as childishly. What else are they to model their behaviours on but our silly mimicry of their own? That said, I believe it's even more than a learned phenomenon. My personal theory is that at some point in our evolutionary history a neural pathway was forged that made the wave an involuntary response to looking like an idiot, or seeing someone like us look that way. When either they or we are in motion, at least two neural pathways are involved. I believe my wave theory completely refutes the theory of intelligent design: if a being who was created in his Creator's image turns into an idiot at the passing of a boat or train or, as in my case, a pilgrim, the Creator, by definition, must also possess sub-genius qualities. A theory of idiotic design, at least in reference to pilgrims waving like idiots, would be more apropos.

I waved like an idiot as I headed out of town. Rita and Fujiko did too. And all the locals waved right back.

THAT NIGHT we were going to be sleeping in church, something some Christians like my brother-in-law get to do every Sunday. But we each would get our own bed because the Church *de la Trinidad*, some years ago, was converted into the municipal *albergue* of Sahagún. A second floor cut the great stained-glass windows in two, dividing the sanctuary into a top and bottom, kind of like heaven and hell, but with hell on top. Downstairs there was a lovely reception area and a beautiful public meeting hall, which it turned out was strictly *for public use only* – no pilgrims allowed. In contrast, the upstairs had a communal bedroom, toilets and adjoining showers, where pilgrims could work on their faith, hope and humidity.

I checked into the *albergue*, even though I was 99% sure I was going to stay at the two-star hotel across the street. But for €3 I bought myself the right to visit my friends without trespassing.

The three of us headed upstairs where the women each chose a bunk. Even though the church had been cut in two, the ceilings still reached halfway to heaven. The top half of the sanctuary afforded a huge open space but partitions separated the rows of bunk beds. Once you got to the confines of your own bed, it actually felt quite private. It was like sitting in your own living room – if your living room was the size of a large crate. If not for the abject lack of heat, the dankness and the darkness, this place would have suited me fine.

Just as I was about to leave to get a hotel room across the street, a group of cyclists arrived. As they did, I was reminded how some of the best scenery we had seen on the Camino had been in the *albergues*. And it had been thanks to cyclists like these, who showed evidence of the almost miraculous effects of regular exercise on the male form.

"If God created man in his own image, God was a cyclist," said Rita.

Watching as one spandexed guy removed his top at the far end of the hall, I figured that 93.4% of the women, along with approximately 9.8% of the men (myself included), could not take their eyes off him. I wondered if it was a venial or a mortal sin to objectify a fellow pilgrim. Whatever it was, enjoying his physical perfection from afar was a spiritual experience. He loitered in a pool of light cast through the top half of a stained glass window, conscious of being admired by all. His shoulders were broad, his chest chiselled and his back muscular and manly. His mighty calves were the size of full grown cows.

As he took his towel and shaving kit out of his panniers, Rita grabbed her toothbrush: "I'm going to brush my teeth."

The young man disappeared into the communal bathroom, with Rita following as stealthily as a birder hoping to catch a closer glimpse of a fabulous bird of paradise.

I breathed a deep sigh and headed for Hotel Alfonso VI (☆☆) across the street. It was made of long thin bricks, mud and hewn timber, but managed to look somewhat unreal, like a pencil drawing. I couldn't tell exactly how old it was but it was certainly older than anybody I knew, including my grandmother, who had recently passed away at 104. I entered through the back door and zigzagged through hallways and additions spanning the Middle Ages and the Renaissance (not to mention the '50s, '60s, '70s and '80s). I checked in and paid in advance and then walked up a flight of stairs to the *first* floor and entered my room, happy for the privacy. It surprised me that, despite walking most of the day alone, I still liked to make time for myself.

Instead of washing my clothes in the sink, I poured shampoo and bath gel into a hot bath, climbed in fully clothed, and scrubbed like crazy with a bar of soap. Still in the tub, I dozed off and enjoyed one of the best sleeps of the Camino. When I woke up, the water was starting to cool, so I climbed out of the tub, disrobed, wrung out my wet clothes and laid them flat on dry towels. Next, I rolled them into the towels as if I was making strudel. Then I stomped on them as if I was crushing grapes to make wine. Most of the water from my clothes ended up in the towels, pretty well guaranteeing that they'd be dry by the next morning. After getting dressed, I opened the large square window at the far end of my room and hung my laundry on a line to dry. As I looked out at all the other square windows, pilgrims and locals alike were doing the same thing. We smiled and waved at each other like idiots.

OVER DINNER, Rita had us look ahead to the next day. As she did, I couldn't help but think of the roles we had each assumed on this walk. Rita managed the stops, the stays and the ways to get there with her guidebook. Fujiko made sure we ate and rested enough, like a doting mother. And then there was me, the translator who was making it up as he went along.

Together we formed a nomadic triumvirate extracting all we could from Spain. We walked its path, ate its food and drank its wine, noting the strangeness of it all, even though we were the foreigners. We were the uninvited guests who for the most part had felt infinitely welcomed.

How to Wash and Dry Pilgrim Laundry

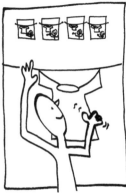

It amazed me how happy the locals seemed to be to have us file interminably past their homes. Not everyone paid attention, to be sure, but an amazing number did. And even though the conversations we had were forced and often one-sided we felt a real connection. In fact, I could imagine buying a house right there, within walking distance of Santiago, when it came time to retire, because I would have so many people to talk to. And if I told the same stories over and over again, so what? The tide of pilgrims never turns. The current flows relentlessly toward Santiago, carrying pilgrims along like driftwood. Every day there would be a new mess of them to talk to, who needed to connect with those rooted in the land.

As much as I liked to think I was self-sufficient, walking across Spain with everything on my back, I was not. I needed their beds, banks, stores, and stories. When I had stopped a shepherd the day before because I found his rustic clothing quaint, I might have looked attentive, but I was greedily listening to his incomprehensible stories hoping to gain an experience to take home with me as a souvenir.

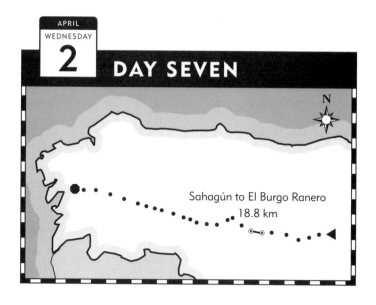

DAY SEVEN

Sahagún to El Burgo Ranero
18.8 km

N

THIS WAS OUR SEVENTH DAY of walking and I felt like we'd gone nowhere. Groups of pilgrims warned us about the Meseta, which some feel is the hardest part of the Camino because it's so flat for so long. It's both a human and scenic vacuum. In contrast to the dearth of visual stimulation, the great plain of the Meseta is known for its quadruple whammy of extremes: heat, cold, wind and nothingness. We'd experienced them all, but the last had been the most challenging.

In the absence of external stimuli, it was almost impossible not to get lost inside myself or to interpret the nothingness around me as a reflection of what I was missing, like gratitude, for example. I'd been wondering what was wrong with me for not wanting to be here. Most people would give almost anything to take four weeks off work for an adventure like this. I felt unthankful, spoiled, superficial or at best shallow. I hadn't said a word about my true feelings to Rita and Fujiko. I'd been walking with a brave pilgrim face.

Nevertheless, there had been a good vibe between us, and the group seemed to have coalesced in these seven days. For one thing, till now, we had shopped only for ourselves and politely refused any offerings made at picnics. From this point on, when we shopped we each assumed a different responsibility. The day before, I had been yogurt and nuts, Rita was meat and bread, Fujiko was fish and fruit. Everyone bought chocolate, and at our picnic, we just poured everything onto the table and dug in as though yours was mine and mine was ours.

Food had been the one bit of sweetness as we had woven our way across this terrain that many pilgrims wished they could avoid. Koreans we met in Burgos told us they were bussing it to León and, at that point, I was feeling jealous. What was taking us nine long days to walk, they likely bussed in a morning. Their guilt, if there was any, was a small price to pay for forgiving themselves of the tedium we were walking through.

RITA WAS APPLYING BANDAGES to her feet as we gathered before heading out. This was something that she did several times a day, and I had taken more than a little interest in it. It was becoming a kind of living geography lesson in fact. Every day the affected regions shifted and grew. On this day, the blister on her heel looked like Scandinavia. I thought that the next day it might swell to become China. And by the time we arrived in Santiago? The world!

Poor Rita. She was in pain and must have been suffering, but she didn't complain. I think she accepted it as part of her journey.

"Today we can choose the meandering but picturesque cake walk through wild meadows, where a pilgrim was bitten by a wolf in 1583, or we can zip along the highway and die of boredom," said Rita, looking up from her guidebook, which was propped open with a box of bandages.

Hmm, which will it be? I wondered, knowing that Rita was about to choose "fast but boring" over "nice but long."

Sure enough, Rita chose a quick death of boredom along highway number A-231. And as I walked, I tried to pretend that the endless drone of traffic was the perfect orchestral score to the visual monotony. Truck drivers blew their horns and waved amicably while cars whizzed by without any notice whatsoever. A toy-sized passenger train, several kilometres away across untilled fields, drew people back to Madrid with a muted buzz. Looking around at the bland uniformity, I was glad for not having brought my camera – it wouldn't have been worth the extra weight.

From time to time, I tried to end the timeless loop playing in my head. I wondered why I couldn't just be glad to be here.

Thoughts like this turned this one-day walk into a week-long journey. In truth, if there was one thing I had learned so far, it's that Christian pilgrimages require a certain Buddhist-like acceptance of how things are rather than how I would like them to be. So, I distracted myself from the war raging inside my head and meditated instead on a certain truth I had seen repeatedly on the Meseta: the dogs here are ugly as sin. To escape the day, I leaned against a rock and wrote a poem in my notebook.

Paul's Doggy Doggerel

Walking amid regions far from Madrid
I spotted something uncouth.
Heaven forbid but the dogs looked like squid
Without legs (and that is the truth).

German shepherds' long legs
Disappeared 'mongst the dregs
While in cities they seemed to have oodles.
And on the Meseta, the proud Irish Setter
Was mated with miniature poodles.

AS WE STOPPED FOR LUNCH at a pilgrim service area called *Virgen de Pirales*, with its very own chapel dedicated to said virgin, a cross between a German shepherd and a slinky was happier to see us than we would have liked. It was not until we succeeded in shooing it away that it became safe for each of us to take a turn "visiting the flowers" behind the chapel. We then sat at the biggest stone picnic table I had ever seen. It could easily have seated 20 feasting pilgrims (28, in a pinch).

We each poured out a stash of food to make one great communal picnic pile of edible odds and ends and leftovers. Then we rummaged for what most caught our fancy. Fujiko was into tinned fish, Rita, lunch meats, while I was momentarily back on the vegetarian wagon. My orange sandwich was so delicious that I jotted down the recipe in my notebook, along with several others.

Paul's Pilgrim Recipes

Orange Sandwich
> Orange
> French-style baguette
> Feta Cheese (see below)

Peel orange. Split baguette in two. Place orange slices in baguette with Feta cheese.

Feta Accompli or
Away-from-Home Homemade Feta
> Tub of Plain Yogurt

Place tub in uppermost pouch of backpack. Walk with sun on back for at least 5 days, or until tub begins to swell. Open tub and smear contents on bread. Actual Greeks will think it's the real McCoy.

Fish & Chips

> Anchovy paste
> Santa Clara brand potato chips
> Newspaper

Fold newspaper into a cone. Fill with potato chips. Smear with anchovy paste. Serves one.

Pilgrim Spanish Omelette Sandwich

    3 Kinder Eggs*

    Leftover baguette

Crack open Kinder Eggs and remove free toys. Set aside. Crush chocolate eggs onto leftover baguette. Eat as you play with toys (optional).

In my normal sedentary life, portion size is always a part of weight control. In fact, I had been thinking of writing a book geared to the North American audience that focuses on just that. Its working title is: *If It's Bigger Than Your Ass, Don't Eat It All In One Sitting.* But on the Camino I was burning so many calories I was literally walking my ass off. I could have eaten my weight in sugar-covered donuts and still not gained a gram. Suddenly it was not enough to eat a balanced diet in the conventional sense. In fact, it was vital to choose foods that were more calorie-dense. So I created a chart related to a balanced pilgrim diet, which I wrote in my notebook.

The Balanced Pilgrim Diet

To create a meal, choose two items from each food group, or if you're walking more than 30 km a day, eat the entire table.

Protein	Grains	Vegetables	Fruit
• Whole chickens • Tins of beans • Peanut butter cups • Pickled herring	• Cake • Donuts • Twinkies • Beer	• Caramel corn • French fries • Potato chips • Vodka	• Merlot • Cabernet Sauvignon • Pinot Grigio • Shiraz

-----

* Kinder Eggs are hollow chocolate eggs with cool toys inside them that often require assembly. They're sold everywhere in the world except the US, because in 1938, the *Federal Food, Drug, and Cosmetic Act* prohibited the inclusion of "non-nutritive" substances in food. Yet junk food is legal? The world is a strange place.

WE FINALLY ARRIVED at El Burgo Ranero in the late afternoon. Rita and Fujiko were drawn to the municipal *albergue*, while I, on the other hand, was drawn to the balconied hotel across the street that had a fabulous view of their misery. My hotel spanned three green doors of a series of stuccoed row houses, which were replicated all the way to the main square about 100 metres on.

That night, we sat in a dining hall that had fine linens and watched a giant flat-screen TV. Our meal lasted as long as *La Rueda de la Fortuna, Cuestión de Peso* and *¿Quién quiere ser Millonario? (Wheel of Fortune, Biggest Loser* and *Who Wants to be a Millionaire.)*

We finished our ice cream that had been served in plastic tubs just as a contestant got the following $64,000 question wrong: What is the quintessential ingredient of a traditional Spanish omelette? A) Cheese B) Tomatoes C) Bread D) Potatoes?

"Potatoes!" we shouted. "Potatoes!"

But it was too late. The poor guy answered, "A) Cheese. Final answer."

Among the last sounds I heard this night were the women giggling as they gathered their laundry on the balcony across the street. The fun stopped when Dolores's voice admonished them with, "Please to be quiet!" This was followed by another rally of giggles. And then silence.

Overhead, the full moon shone brightly. Somewhere, a faceless stubby little Spanish dog howled pathetically.

DAY EIGHT

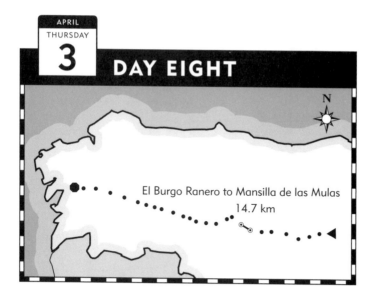

N

El Burgo Ranero to Mansilla de las Mulas
14.7 km

AS FUJIKO SERVED US JAPANESE SNACKS she'd been carrying for eight days, I tried to make sense of the seemingly endless supply of everything in her backpack. Rita and I had talked about it. At first, we thought it was because she was an experienced hiker and had climbed 100 mountains, including Mount Kilimanjaro and France's Mont Blanc. But then, it had started to get a little spooky. In addition to her own things, Fujiko had offered me Chinese tea and pills, bandages, an extra towel, a flashlight, and at this point, one of those spoon-knife-fork contraptions aptly called a spork. She had offered Rita a second hat, a blouse and a scarf. In Burgos, she gave painkillers to an ailing Frenchman we met on the street. And when a Korean named Ronald was suffering from shin splints, she actually reached for her pack and asked, "Shall I make a cast?"

"Fujiko is like a Japanese Mary Poppins," said Rita.

And everything Fujiko had, she shared. That's why Rita and I made a pact to track all the things we saw enter or leave Fujiko's pack. I even wrote a list in my notebook.

Unusual Things in Fujiko's Pack

(or why we thought Fujiko was a Japanese Mary Poppins)

Truly Mary Poppins:
Formal white gloves
Tons of sweets (from both the East and the West)
Miniature black umbrella that opens up wide
Two extra sporks
American Airlines First Class salt & pepper shakers (real china)

Unusual and Sort of Mary Poppins:
Huge sunhat
A pharmacy worth of pills (from both the East and the West)
White surgical mask (Is she also a doctor?)
Metal mat (For performing surgery? For frying eggs? Not sure)
Extra set of towels
Tissues (She never seemed to run out, and I never saw her
    buy any)
Matches from Best Western Hotel Atlántico
    (She doesn't smoke)
Plastic beach sandals (blue)
String and rope (about 1 metre each)

Typically Japanese:
Three pairs of toe socks (They're still popular in Japan)
Electronic translator (Manages six languages)
Two Thermoses (Most pilgrims just use recyclable water bottles)
White bandana (with Buddhist sutra written on it)
Book (The Life of Buddha)

After we got our fill of Fujiko's Japanese snacks and cookies, she held up more saying, "Aren't you hungry?"

We held our stomachs and pleaded with her for mercy.

THE MORNING'S PATH was lined with plane trees all the way to the horizon. They stood along this part of the Camino at eight-meter intervals, thanks to a tree-planting grant from UNESCO. They were not the twisted arthritic plane trees that reached ominously across our path in Burgos, which joined hands overhead. These trees stood polite and upright – like real professionals. Looking at them, I could imagine how it might soon be possible to walk all the way to Santiago in the shade, once they managed to spread their canopies. The path (or *senda*) had also received money from UNESCO. It was made of white gravel and was so smooth that you could drive a small car on it.

As I walked along, I thought how UNESCO's generosity had both improved and destroyed this part of the Camino. The trail was so perfect as to be devoid of feeling, and made the authentic pilgrim experience feel contrived. The manicured trail cut the Meseta in two and left me feeling detached from the real world on either side. As much as I like my luxury, I couldn't help but wonder how boring it would be if UNESCO smoothed out every wrinkle. I'd likely complain that it wasn't real enough, and I'd miss how involved I feel when I have things to struggle against. Without so much as a stone to twist my ankle on, I found myself tuning out.

Around 1 p.m., the Camino turned northwest: we started walking toward the distant mountains and, about 40 minutes later, we arrived at train tracks. The road allowed us to go under and we passed a wall of graffiti.

Graffiti on Day Eight

Spanish	English
Carlos + Lucia	Carlos + Lucia
Stop Guerra Irak!	Stop the War in Iraq
País Lionés Libre	A Free Country of León

"What does it mean?" asked Fujiko.

"From what I gather, Carlos loves Lucia so much that he wants to stop the war in Iraq so he can start one in Spain."

Once we arrived on the far side of the tracks, the mountains seemed exponentially closer than they had just moments earlier. As we approached Mansilla de las Mulas, they stood ever taller, revealing more of their rocky faces: wrinkles, crags, cliffs and all. They looked steep, wild, dangerous and exceptionally beautiful.

We walked into Mansilla de las Mulas around 2:30, following shells of polished brass on stone walkways. We found *Albergue de Peregrinos* along one of the many cobblestone arteries reaching out from the main square in all directions. Once again, the manager's name was Jesus and his photo actually appeared in Fujiko's Japanese guidebook.

He greeted us in both English and Japanese, stamped our pilgrim passports, and said, "You will meet angels on the Camino." Then he paused before adding, "You ... are *my* angels."

Jesus tapped a finger on a deck of cards: "Please choose an angel card,"* he said.

Oh, for God's sake, I thought to myself. (But I took one anyway.)

Fujiko drew "Transformation," Rita drew "Honesty", and I drew "Synthesis."

"Shoot! I was hoping for *"Photo*synthesis," I joked.

As we went to put back our cards, Jesus said, "No, they are for you to keep."

Rita and Fujiko seemed really pleased, but I couldn't help but think how I was going to have to lug this thing all the way to Santiago. Returning it, I said, "Thank you, but my backpack is already too heavy."

Rita rolled her eyes.

"But Paul-*san*†," said Fujiko. "It is your gardening angel!"

"I insist," said Jesus.

I accepted the card with a smile, while wishing I had the courage to tell Jesus I didn't believe.

----

* Angel cards look like regular playing cards except they are designed to catapult meaningless existences into ones replete with cosmic intention (one word at a time).

† The suffix "*san*" is a gender-neutral Japanese honorific used to show respect. Think Mr., Mrs., Ms. and Miss all rolled into one.

THE *ALBERGUE DE PEREGRINOS* was housed in what appeared to have been the primary residence of a wealthy member of the medieval merchant class. It had a kitchen, a modest foyer and stairs, bathrooms and reception. An open door led to a courtyard, which Fujiko's guidebook stated "is the place where pilgrims meet." No one was meeting there on this day, as it was undergoing major renovations.

Upstairs, the many dorm-style rooms were found off a windowed hallway that wound its way around the courtyard like a mountain road. Fujiko darted in and out of the various bedrooms scouting out the best possible room for us to get the best possible rest. She chose the smallest one (maximum capacity: four) and we quickly spread out our belongings to discourage anyone from joining us.

With our own private business attended to, we left the quiet of our room and entered into the beehive-like busyness of the *albergue*, where pilgrims attended to their own private business in community, including bathing in cold showers, shaving before unlit mirrors, scrubbing clothes clean in bathroom sinks, preparing and eating food in the kitchen, journaling, drinking, or resting wherever a sympathetic nook could be found. After hanging my laundry in the courtyard where two men were laying bricks, I headed back inside to find the toilets. I opened the first door, marked *"Aseos"** and found the same two men peering at me over a half-finished brick wall.

«¿*Donde* is the *aseos?*» I asked.

The men said something helpful that was hopelessly lost on me. I closed the door and opened another, as if I was starring in a Spanish farce. The next door opened to what I believe was the one toilet available for the 65 pilgrims staying there.

The afternoon slipped by without incident – well, there were actually two. First, a shopkeeper, in one of the many Spanish cigarette shops where the Spanish also sell stamps, tried to

---

* "Aseos" means toilets and it's easy to remember because it sounds like what you sit on when you're there.

cheat Fujiko out of the change she was owed. He won't try that again. And second, poor Rita learned the hard way that she was in a particular part of Spain where it is absolutely imperative when buying a particular traditional Spanish cake to weigh the thing before carrying it to the cash for purchase.

"I don't know why the lady was all *«La la la la la la la»* about it," Rita said, finishing the last creamy bits, icing sugar paling her rosy cheeks in the sun's last rays before dinner.

ON THIS NIGHT, we had decided we were going to eat like the locals and enjoy a traditional Spanish meal. So we were obviously excited when we found a restaurant serving *comida de la tierra*. The locals must be eating in tonight, we thought, because the place was empty except for the three of us and the runny-nosed waitress, who looked too hardy to ever catch a cold. She walked us directly into the kitchen to see for ourselves what the Spanish eat on a regular basis, and then asked us, "Is it good?"

«Si, si, si», we said in unison. We would soon see that *«No, no, no»* could have alleviated so much unnecessary human suffering.

As the dust in the courtyard settled into darkness, the waitress arrived with three plates and two bottles of wine (one of each species). She placed it all in front of us, and we then tried to decipher the different mounds by poking them with our forks.

"Cabbage," I said.

"Chick peas," said Fujiko.

"Blood sausage!" said Rita, which made me spit something red out of my mouth and over her left shoulder.

"Blood sausage?" I repeated. "I'm not eating that."

"How's the wine?" asked Rita, trying to focus on something more positive.

"If the locals make wonderful wines, they're not sharing any with us," I grumbled. "I hope the red is better."

When we were through, the waitress gave us our bill, as well as a guest book for us to sign, which she handed to Fujiko.

So as to disguise the sarcasm, Fujiko wrote the following in Japanese: "Thank you for the authentic Spanish experience."

Rita wrote, "A meal I will tell everyone about – including my therapist."

I wrote, "All four food groups generously misrepresented."

WHEN WE RETURNED to the *albergue*, giddy from our authentic Spanish experience, the lights were already out. We did our best to contain our laughter, which only made it completely uncontainable.

"Please to be quiet," said Dolores's voice from somewhere in the darkness.

Rita and Fujiko instantly stopped laughing. I, on the other hand, couldn't stop. And all the wine, the laughing, and the simple act of returning home had filled me with a prodigious need to pee. I threw open the wrong door and collided with the brick wall the men had been laying earlier (which was now complete – floor-to-ceiling). "Ouch!"

Laughing uncontrollably, Rita and Fujiko disappeared into the only *aseos* and locked the door behind them. I listened to them giggle for five endless minutes and heard the toilet flush twice. When they came out, I was holding my groin as if applying a tourniquet to a severed limb.

When I joined them upstairs, Fujiko had strapped her Mount Fuji headlight to her forehead and was shining it on someone sleeping in the bed above mine. Rita was swooning like a fairytale princess and trying not to laugh. As I closed the door to our room behind me, I could see, lying in a small pool of golden light, a handsome cyclist. That night, I fell asleep feeling a little bit closer to God.

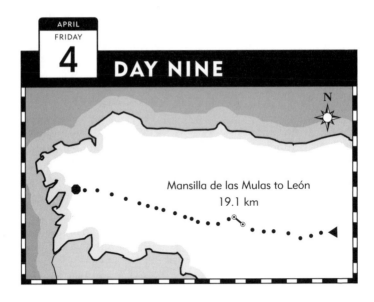

Mansilla de las Mulas to León
19.1 km

"WHAT ARE WE GOING TO DO?" I asked.

"The guidebook doesn't show an alternate route," said Rita, pointing to page 201.

To cross the Río Porma, we had no choice but to cross a narrow bridge that we would be sharing with rush-hour traffic. It was one of the few times that the Spanish seemed rushed, and on this morning it felt downright dangerous. The sky was still black and headlights blinded us as they careened past, replaced instantly by others.

Is it any wonder that I'm often hesitant to jump right in? I thought to myself.

Eighteen-wheelers whizzed by, an arm's length away from us. Dumbfounded, I glanced down to examine the thin white line, which was the only thing that separated me from the final judgment. Up ahead, the shoulder disappeared completely and we were forced to step briefly into oncoming traffic. As we waited for momentary breaks in the flow of vehicles, we each mentally rehearsed how we would run blindly, screaming like schoolgirls – which we subsequently did in turn, some of us more convincingly than others.

Safely on the far side of the bridge, hearts still pounding, Rita gave us the good news: "That bridge was just a dress rehearsal. Before León, we have to cross a four-lane highway."

AT 11:04, WE ARRIVED at the four-lane highway, where cars were speeding by at 140 km an hour. Guessing I could only do about 20, I realized this could quickly get messy.

"I go first," said Fujiko.

"Okay," I said, figuring I might learn something from her mistakes.

Like an Olympic diver poised at the edge of the board, Fujiko placed her toes on the white line indicating the shoulder of the highway. She looked both ways. Then she leapt decisively, propelling her body to the other side in seconds, where she stood proudly, as if waiting for the judges' scores to appear on the nearby *Bimbo Breads* billboard.

"I'll go next," said Rita. She looked both ways and trotted comfortably to the other side, just as a bright red Volvo zoomed past.

It was my turn. I stepped up to the edge of the highway. In the quiet moments that followed, I knew the pilgrim thing to do was to place myself trustingly in God's hands. But frankly, it wasn't as though God had miraculously appeared to hold up a stop sign, blow a whistle and wave me across. From where I was standing, it looked pretty much like it was every man for himself, thank you very bloody much. I was on my own.

Fifteen seconds later, the highway cleared, and I began my life-or-death dash across. But as I did, my sunhat blew off. Without missing a beat, I pivoted, retraced my steps, snatched the hat in mid-air and pivoted again to head back across the highway without so much as looking left or right to see if the coast was still clear.

What is it with the Spanish? I thought to myself. Don't they care at all about safety? Are they so sure of everlasting life that they can afford to squander this one? But then, locals weren't scrambling to cross the highway, only pilgrims. I suppose I should have been asking myself whether I believed in life after...

Just then, I spotted Spain's tiniest automobile coming up the hill, headed straight for me. The car was a blue Santana Motors 1.9L *Stella*, although to refer to it as a car is a tad misleading. It's more like a sewing machine on wheels. But it was headed straight for me. With Fujiko and Rita cheering me on, I ran even more convincingly than before and arrived safely on the other side.

YOU CAN'T KNOW how small a big European city is, I decided, until you walk through its antiseptic suburbs, the wilderness of its industrial parks and then to its vibrant urban core. Walking at a comfortable pace, we made it from the highway to the centre in about one hour and ten minutes. The walk, albeit shorter than you might think, only seemed longer for the dreary monotony and general lack of aesthetic on the outer rim.

The monotony though, afforded me time to think, so think I did. I thought about Jesus – the guy who ran the *albergue* in Boadilla del Camino. And I thought about the other Jesus too – the guy who ran the hostel in Mansilla de las Mulas. Why was Jesus suddenly so much a part of my everyday life, I wondered. After a bit of thought, I figured it was because the Spanish are simply comfortable naming their kids after their Lord and Saviour. Not that they think their brats are better than the next guy's. After all, their neighbours are naming their kids Jesus too. So much so that Jesus is all but running rampant in Spain. In fact, if you stand on a corner and say, "Jesus is coming," people think you mean "for dinner," because everybody in Spain is either named Jesus, has a friend named Jesus, or knows somebody who knows Jesus personally. There is even a town called Jesus. (Parents that live there phone their kids at Christmas saying, "Come home to Jesus, Jesus.")

The Spanish mean no disrespect in any of this. It just never became taboo to use the Lord's name in vain, or for financial gain either. As we walked into town, I noticed five *"Jesus"* businesses, which I jotted down in my notebook.

Jesus Businesses

- *Casa Jesus* (A Spanish house of pancakes)
- *Jesus Pastor* (Kitchen stuff)
- *Joyería Jesus Lòpez* (Jewellery and bling)
- *Agencia de Viajes Jesus* (Travel agency)
- *Comestibles ma Jesus* (Edible things Jesus)

At 12:24, I stopped and asked a man for directions to Hotel Paris (☆☆☆) and it was uncanny how much Spanish I understood.

"Go to the end of this street and turn right," he gestured.

I led the group to the end of the street. We turned and about 100 metres further down, we were standing in front of Hotel Paris (☆☆☆) like runaways returning home.

"I'm going to spend the rest of the day in a tub," said Rita, going in first.

"O saki ni," I said to Fujiko, which is a time-honoured sign of respect that means, "I go first."* Fujiko entered last, the heavy glass door closing slowly behind her.

Later, we met for dinner and managed to get the last outdoor table at the micro-brewery next door. Whereas in Canada waiters wait on you, in Spain their job seems to be to make *you* wait. From what I gathered, the relaxed attitude was supposed to be infectious. But it took me a while to buy into this *laissez-faire* attitude.

In any case, as we waited to be served, we watched thousands of people parade along *Calle Ancha*, the stylish pedestrian

---

* Used only by Japanese men cutting in front of women. Japanese women have not developed a way of showing equal respect to men. I kept meaning to ask Fujiko if they were working on it.

walkway that Hotel Paris (☆☆☆) is on. A man danced with his three-year-old daughter in front of an accordion player. Another man, dressed as a ballerina, caroused with his drinking buddies and wove in and out of bars. Two elderly women in wheelchairs rolled through town. Street performers set up, performed and struck their shows as crowds gathered and dispersed. Unlicensed street vendors did the same, scattering only when police patrols of three arrived. Parents walked, talked and laughed with their teenagers, repeatedly stopping to kiss both cheeks, or air around those cheeks, of friends.

Once the waiter decided we had waited long enough, Rita ordered Spanish tapas mentioned in her guidebook, and *slowly*, our faith in Spanish cuisine was restored.

WHEN WE GOT BACK to our rooms, it was nearly midnight. Comatose, I collapsed on my bed only to be woken up three-quarters of an hour later by a terrible ruckus outside. I stepped onto the balcony and saw thousands of people still on the street.

Was it a revolution? Or was León already free?

Over the next several hours the mob got louder. Men on the street were slurring their speech, shouting things that sounded really stupid and then laughing uproariously. Around 3 a.m. they played street soccer, substituting an empty restaurant-sized tub of ice cream for the ball. As the game waned, the steady staccato of stilettos clicked up and down *Calle Ancha*, like an over-sexed metronome. Women were on the street, collecting their men, whether they belonged to them or not. Shortly after, an army of street cleaners arrived in trucks that beep-beep-beeped in reverse. There was the spray of water and the banging of garbage bins being righted, emptied and put back in place. Then, just before sunrise, there was a powerful clanging of metal on metal.

Someone was breaking into Jesus Lòpez' jewellery shop!

But when I looked outside, it was just the gas company fixing something that couldn't possibly wait until morning.

At 7:36, there was civil twilight.

At 8:05, the actual sunrise.

And at 8:10, I climbed into a hot bath, calculating that I got 45 minutes of sleep at a cost of one euro per minute.

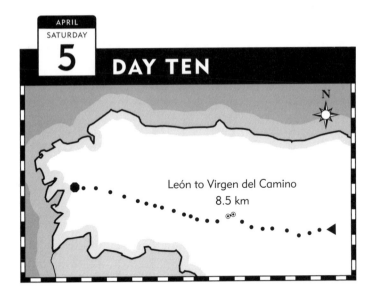

DAY TEN

León to Virgen del Camino
8.5 km

RITA HAD GIVEN US THE MORNING OFF and I was thrilled to have it all to myself. We weren't leaving until 2 p.m., as she had scheduled an easy 8.5-km walk to a nearby suburb.

"You're going to want to sleep in, see the sights and run errands," Rita said the night before.

How right she was. Top of the list for me was to ship things home that I didn't need, like underwear. When I was kept awake by the street-party-nobody-invited-me-to the night before, I couldn't stop thinking about how my backpack was still way too heavy. I need to lighten my load, I had thought to myself. And that's when I decided to ship home my skivvies.

So I found myself at the main post office of León just after it opened. I had a green express envelope and was stuffing it with two pairs of black Calvin Klein briefs. The clerk on the other side of the counter pretended not to notice, weighed the parcel and then handed me a customs form on which she had written that I was shipping home 70 grams of sexy underwear.*

----

* *"Ropa interior erótica*: 70 g".

Back on the steps of the post office, I stood with legs apart, hands on hips, feeling a cool morning breeze. I was 5,619 km from home, I had gone commando and felt freer than I had in years. Well, in truth, I was not exactly as free as all that, but I was freer than I had been. My water-resistant hiking pants actually came with their own built-in underwear.

When I first discovered this, I thought, Yuk. And so I had brought some extras just in case. But the built-ins had actually worked out well. If more men knew about them, everything from GUESS jeans to Giorgio Armani dress pants would be retro-fitted with built-ins. They'd even end up in kilts.

Next, I headed to the department store where I bought a pair of black waterproof rain pants, feeling cheated that they didn't come with their own underwear.

AT JUST AFTER TWO IN THE AFTERNOON, Rita and Fujiko were waiting for me patiently in the lobby. We left Hotel Paris (☆☆☆) and turned on *Calle Ancha*. After about 100 metres, the street opened to the square, where the Santa María de León Cathedral rose up from the pavement to the heavens, taking our breath with it. A masterpiece of Gothic architecture, it glowed with golden hues. It was like a giant sandcastle, newly carved, whose exquisite detail had not yet been worn away by wind or waves.

Rita gasped: "How do you not believe in God? I mean, we all have imagination but this is incredible."

The interior of the cathedral was as dark as the exterior was bright. Sheets of black plastic hung from scaffolding, concealing the magnificent stained glass windows and preventing daylight from shining on the cathedral floor.* Huge columns rose from the gloom like mighty redwoods reaching for the sun.

After wandering about, I found myself in a small side chapel, one of the many places of worship lining the outer

---

* The plastic over the windows, it turns out, was to prevent sunlight from shining on the floor and cracking the foundation. Who would have thought?

walls of the sanctuary. Inside, several elderly women were kneeling silently in prayer.

Under a statue of the Blessed Virgin, my religious experience came by way of electric and not real candles – a first. It cost me 50 centimes* but it was worth it to see five flame-shaped light bulbs shine just for me. I made a wish feeling a little guilty for not taking the electric candles more seriously. But my wish was sincere nonetheless. I wished that I could learn to stop arguing with life, and to accept it as it is.

As I left the side chapel, heading back into the nave of the cathedral, I held the door for an old Spaniard. He accepted the courtesy but then spoke angrily and pointed to a sign that read: "NOT GO IN EXCEPT FOR PRAYING."

Wait a minute, I thought to myself. Wishes are prayers too. Wishes are prayers that respect the fact that God has a billion things to do at any given moment and don't ask Him to snap to it right away. Wishes also make us sound less needy, and, given how busy He is, the Almighty must appreciate those who help themselves.

I stepped back into the nave and took a moment. Although I was raised Catholic, I've never felt at home in the Roman Catholic Church, except for a brief period in Grade 3 when I would step off the bus and head straight into Sacred Heart Church every morning before school. There in the first pew, I'd meet my friend Harry. Together, he and I would celebrate an abridged version of Mass, as life-sized stone statues of Mary, Joseph, and lesser saints, placed strategically around the church, eyed the two of us like prayer wardens. My father's Romanian parents prayed earnestly to these statues, and I tried to do my best, too. But looking at them, I never felt anything but empty, cold, and confused. Instead of connecting me with the Almighty, they telegraphed the absolute ordinariness of life.

That's why I was so grateful for Father Morel. He was *extraordinary*, and turned the Mass into theatre. Even if it wasn't his intent, I was grateful to him because he awakened something in me that felt real and alive. Because of him, five

---
* Think 50 cents, then multiply by 1.6244.

mornings a week began with drama, comedy, mystery and magic. Mass started with a vital sense of urgency as Father Morel entered, reciting the Mass from the back of the church. Then he processed so quickly up the aisle I figured he was wearing roller skates under his cassock. He ran off his lines like the ecclesiastical equivalent of a modern Major-General. Whenever the choir sang, he continued speaking, his large gestures always attracting our attention. Mass ended when Father Morel waved the sign of the cross in the air like he was shooing us away. Then he rattled off the final blessing as he retreated into the vestry.

He was amazing. Whereas it can take 30 minutes to bake a cake, Father Morel managed to turn bread and wine into the body and blood of Christ in just under 20. In his hands, the transubstantiation* was magic.

It was the part of the Mass that proved to me that, unlike the statues, God was a real, albeit extraordinary person. I can thank the bells for that. As the bread and wine were converted into the body and blood of Jesus Christ, high-pitched ethereal bells rang. Their exquisite tinkling seemed angelic – a divine magic. They told me God was as real as Harry seated next to me. They washed away the empty feelings I felt from the statues until, that is, the day that I noticed an altar boy pick up and ring a set of tiny brass bells. I was profoundly shaken. Naïvely, I had believed the ringing to be supernatural. Suddenly I was left with some very big questions: If God needs a kid to ring his bells, how real can God be? And in what other ways does He need people to prop Him up?

Sadly, I stopped meeting Harry in church, although I continued to go with the family on Sundays. But once I moved out and could decide things for myself, I found other things to do on Sunday mornings.

As I left the Santa María de León Cathedral through the small wooden door-within-a-door of the main entrance, I banged my head and cursed under my breath. Then, I lost

---

* Transubstantiation, in the Roman Catholic Faith, is where the bread and wine of communion are *transubstantiated* into the actual body and blood of Christ.

myself in a crowd of gaping tourists standing in the square looking up.

I wondered, if God didn't exist, why we would build this? And then thought, if God existed, would we need to build it?

IN LARGER CITIES, where the local economy is not dependent on 100,000 pilgrims walking through town spending money as they go, the locals took very little interest in us. And so we walked out of León unnoticed and in silence, past children playing ball on the street, past couples walking their dogs and past old men pushing baby carriages.

We walked through the furniture district promising *venta directa de fábrica* ("sales direct from the factory"). Three-metre-long yellow arrows did nothing but confuse us, as they were not meant for pilgrims. They didn't point to Santiago but rather to discount outlets, where we could, if we wanted, pick up a sofa at 50% off and carry it on our backs the rest of the way, putting it down, from time to time, to rest on it from all the extra weight.

Once past the furniture district, we began a long steep climb through the poorer suburbs and entered an industrial wasteland of empty lots and deserted warehouses, leaving León and its towering cathedral in the valley below.

Eventually the Camino reconnected with the highway that we had earlier crossed and we then walked into Virgen del Camino. The suburb is famous for its church of modern miracles, named after San Froilán. As we arrived, hundreds of people were congregating for the four o'clock Mass. (In today's day and age, that in itself is a miracle.) As people entered, they waved the sign of the cross over their foreheads or across their chests. Then they touched idols carved into the brass doors for luck and blessings. The shiniest and hence the luckiest icons to rub included San Froilán's face, a dead man's skull, a seashell, the "ó" in "León," as well as several shiny things that had been rubbed down to unrecognizable blobs of supreme good fortune.

As we entered, Rita said the rectangular church was built in 1961 in a modern style, and so resembled an oversized shoebox.

White light streamed through the small rectangular windows above us into the unadorned interior like tissue paper. It enveloped the minimalist altar as if it were wrapping a shiny new shoe. Although miracles are said to happen here all the time, crutches rendered redundant did not line the walls as one might expect. It was as if invalids were restored on a strictly carry-in-carry-out basis.

Out front, lining the facade, the great bronze statues of San Froilán, Mary and the apostles were stretched exaggeratedly heavenward. The statue of San Froilán was poised with three fingers in the air as if he had just licked them and was checking the wind speed and direction to determine if current meteorological conditions were safe for Mary's assumption, or if it would be prudent to postpone it another day.

Across from the entrance to the church and a few steps down, we discovered the San Froilán Souvenir and Gift Shop. It turned out to be the Walmart of ecclesiastical boutiques.

"Jeez," said Rita. "The closer to God, the gaudier it gets."

I wrote a list of the most unusual items for sale, wondering if they could also be purchased on-line.

For Sale in the San Froilán Souvenir and Gift Shop

- Pope Benedict XVI action figure. Rome's version of GI Joe.
- Mini beer mugs. So boys can be men when they play with the pope.
- Cigarette lighters. For those who can't wait to meet their maker.
- Santa Claus manger scene. Includes Jesus, Mary, Santa, tree, toys and elves.

THAT NIGHT, I dreamed of being submerged in water at the house by the lake where my grandparents lived. The family room was flooded. All that was visible was the top of the sofa and the top of my head. The family ate dinner in the dining room without me, eyed by a framed portrait of Jesus wearing a T-shirt that read, "Only 160 more shopping days until Christmas."

DAY ELEVEN

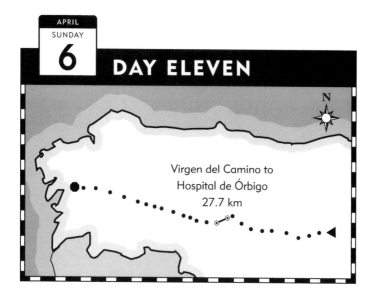

Virgen del Camino to
Hospital de Órbigo
27.7 km

AS THE SUN CAME UP, I saw that wild mustard along the path was covered with frost, and looked like lettuce placed too close to the back of the fridge. Rather than admit that I wished I had warmer clothes, I suggested we stop as soon as we could for breakfast. Within 3 km of starting out, we found an *albergue* which was so large, so new, and so clean that it felt like a four-star hotel (albeit where everybody sleeps in the same room). Famished as always, we ordered Spanish omelette.

«¡You are *ayujadora!*» I said to the young owner as she returned soon after with our food.

She blushed and laughed sweetly.

"*Ayujadora*" is a Spanish word I made up. It means "a very helpful woman". In Spanish, there is a word "*trabajadora*" which means a woman who works a lot. I just applied the same ending, "*jadora*" to the root of the word "*ayudar*" (to help) and voilà: "*Ayujadora*" and instant rapport! The woman's response inspired me. I suddenly wanted to help my fellow pilgrims connect more with the locals. Over the next 24 km, I stopped here

and there to draft PAUL'S INCOMPLETE GUIDE TO PIL-
GRIM SPANISH in my notebook.

Paul's Incomplete Guide to Pilgrim Spanish

PRONUNCIATION
As selfish as it might seem, the Spanish have little thought for
us when they open their mouths and speak in ways that only
they understand.

The Letters "G" and "J"
The Spanish pronounce the letters "G" and "J" as though they
have gone into anaphylactic shock. (Pronounced gutturally
"Kh-h-h-h," while vibrating that dangly thing at the back of
your throat.) If you say *"trabajadora"* and an American quickly
comes over and performs the Heimlich Manoeuvre on you,
you've got it right.

The Letter "H"
Although the Spanish do not pronounce the letter "H," they
still insist on having one.

The Letter "S"
The Spanish have a soft spot for sibilance, as expressed
through the Castilian lisp. The more pronounced the lisp, the
more authentic the Castilian. Whether it's from belly dancers or
conquistadors, "S" is pronounced "th."

The Letter "C"
The above applies equally to the letter "C" before an "E" or "I"
and the letter "Z."

The Letter "V"
Pronounced "B" as in "bat." "Virgin" in Spanish is *"virgen,"*
but is pronounced "birgen."

COGNATES
Cognates are words so similar in Spanish as in English that
only a moron could not tell what they mean. Here is what I
hope will be an ego-building list.

adventure – *aventura*
catastrophe – *catástrofe*
direction – *dirección*
fatigue – *fatiga*
hotel – *hotel*
imagine – *imaginar*
participation – *participación*
reality – *realidad*
transformation – *transformación*

WORD ENDINGS

Adverbs often end in "*mente.*" For example:
absolutely – *absolutamente*
finally – *finalmente*
immediately – *inmediatamente*

But try also:

English	Wrong but Close Enough	Spanish
assiduously	assiduously-*mente*	*asiduamente*
favourably	favourably-*mente*	*favorablemente*
unexpectedly	unexpectedly-*mente*	*de forma imprevista*

Spanish nouns often end in "encia." Replicate the above technique to invent useful words such as bread-encia, butter-encia and even spork-encia.

PLEASE NOTE: As you can see from the above examples, the Spanish take many English words and make them their own by simply adding longer, fancier endings. This is because they get all romantic over the sound of their mother tongue. It is ill-advised to interrupt Spaniards before their final "*encia*" or "*mente.*" If you do, they may well add longer and fancier endings to things they already said, complicating matters even more.

> Generally speaking, if it takes you longer to say it in Spanish, your Spanish is good.

USEFUL PHRASES – LOCATIONS

Where is the post office?
¿Donde está la oficina de correos?

When is the bloody thing open?
¿Cuando está abierta esta oficina de mierda?

Use also with:
bank – *banco*
supermarket – *supermercado*
hardware store – *ferretería*
bakery – *panadería*

USEFUL PHRASES FOR MAKING FRIENDS

Your dog has really short legs.
Su perro tiene patas cortas.

Easy on the chorizo tomorrow; you are farting in your
sleep again.
*Mañana, no comes tanto chorizo; de nuevo estas echando
pedos cuando duermes.*

Your big toe looks really bad. Stop walking or cut it off. Can I
help you?
*El aspecto de su dedo gordo del pie no es bueno. Parese o
amputelo. ¿Puedo ayudarle?*

THE END

A SHORT 24 KM LATER and I could see that my guide to pilgrim
Spanish was going to come in handy. In the shadowy inner
courtyard of the parish hostel of Hospital de Órbigo sat an old
Spanish woman who looked like she was born with a cigarette
in her mouth.

"I got this," I volunteered, as I approached the woman to
register.

«Hola», I said.

«La la la la la la la-mente», she replied, filtering the evening
air through her cigarette.

«La la la la, la la la la-encia», she added, over-enunciating
this time.

«*¿Qué?*» I asked.

"What is she saying?" asked Rita.

"I'm not sure. She has a very particular accent."

"That would be a Spanish accent," Rita deadpanned.

«*Credenciales por favor*», said the lady, suddenly speaking a Spanish I could understand.

We handed her our pilgrim passports and she stamped them in between heavy puffs.

After handing them back, she asked, «*¿Cuales son sus nombres?*»

«*Tres*», I said.

The old lady rolled her eyes.

«Our *nombres* is *tres*», I repeated, counting us off: "One. Two. Three."

«*¿Cuales son sus nombres?*» she repeated.

"Maybe she's hard of hearing," I said to Rita.

«*¡Sus nombres!*» she repeated again.

«*¡Tre-e-e-es!*» I repeated louder, drawing it out so she would understand.

Putting her hand on my shoulder, Rita said calmly in my right ear, "I think she wants to know our names."

"Yes," said Fujiko, holding her electronic translator. "In Spanish, *nombre* means name. N-O-M-B-R-E. 'Name.'"

«*Sus nombres, por favor*», puffed the woman, wryly smiling.

"Fujiko," recited Fujiko: "F U..."

The old lady stared blankly at her.

"F U...," repeated Fujiko.

"F U...," repeated Fujiko louder.

Rita and I exchanged glances. A tear rolled down her cheek.

"I have an idea-*encia*," I said. «*¿Write-o our nombres?*»

«*Si*», said the old woman, passing the book over to me across the tiny table.

As I wrote our names in her book, the old woman told us where everything was, while pointing in a zillion different directions.

"Got that?" asked Rita when the lady was done, to which I said, «*Nada*».

DAY TWELVE

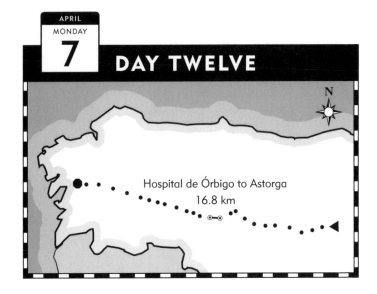

N

Hospital de Órbigo to Astorga
16.8 km

WE MET AT THE WOODEN TABLE in the inner courtyard before dawn. It was cold.

"You forget sleeping bag," said Fujiko, noticing it was still on the table.

"Is there a sack race to Astorga that I should know about?" asked Rita.

"I got an idea in the middle of the night," I said. "Watch!"

Holding my sleeping bag by one end, I inserted one arm with one sleeping bag end through a sleeve of my raincoat. I did the same thing on the other side with the other end, eventually inserting both arms and sleeping bag ends through both sleeves. Then I zipped up my raincoat, stuffing the bulk of the sleeping bag into it, like a scarecrow filling itself with straw.

"Ta-dah!"

"You look like a stork with a beer belly," said Rita.

"I might look silly but, at no extra cost, I have myself a winter coat. And I'm carrying no extra weight."

"Clever boy!" said Fujiko.
"You've gotta work with what you've got."

How To Make a Winter Coat

With Mount Fuji headlights strapped to our heads, we crossed the stony courtyard and stepped through the small door to the street, leaving it open for the morning rush of pilgrims, and then turned onto the main street and headed out of town. It might have been black but the air was lovely and cool.

"It's easier to be fresh when the day is too," said Rita.

"I totally agree," I said, feeling cozy in my new coat, an ingenious invention that only cost me $420 for the raincoat plus $275 for the sleeping bag, plus applicable taxes.*

AFTER A BREAK in a hillside forest, the Camino led us across private property and through a dairy farm, where we were escorted by two neurotic mutts that were a cross between sheepdogs and footstools in need of reupholstering. Intermittently they ran at us, heads low, yapping madly. Then they beetled off, tail between legs, looking back at us with doleful eyes, as if to say, "Sorry about that, we can't help ourselves. We're inbred."

Once we were a safe distance away, they mustered the courage to charge again, repeating this manic affront until the far edge of their domain. Not that I could see any reason to fight for this farm. It was overrun with mud and smelled rank, as if they were making vinegar out of manure.

After climbing for another 10 minutes through a meadow of short grass and spring flowers, we neared the crest of the hill. We saw oaks cleaved to the hillside and discovered the perfect place for a picnic breakfast. Over time, pilgrims had added their piece to create what had become an organic place to commemorate God above and communicate with pilgrims below. There was a three-metre crucifix, a makeshift altar made of pebbles glued to a wooden frame, and a scarecrow dressed as a pilgrim, standing in attendance. Comments in black indelible marker were scribbled on everything from the scarecrow's raincoat, to rocks, pieces of wood and even bits of paper, wedged into crannies or placed under stones so as not to blow away. Messages had also been carved mercilessly into tree trunks with knives and/or sporks.

----

* Good sleeping bags start at around $35/100 g. Mine cost $45.29/100 g and was worth every penny. Raincoats cost a whopping three times that. The one I bought was $106.91/100 g – roughly the same price as silver. Only gold, it seems, is more expensive than pilgrim gear.

I jotted down several in my notebook:

On a rock next to the scarecrow:
God is love and whoever is in love is in God.

Carved in a tree
www.bahai.org

On a rock by the stone altar
Jesus was here

"Damn, we missed Him!" said Rita.

After packing our gear, we continued up the hill and soon found ourselves threading a narrow clay path through dwarfed oak trees. Most of the oaks were still clinging to a full complement of last fall's leaves, as though they had not learned to let go of the past. Bushes, scattered about, had just opened their soft spring buds and stood brilliantly at about a quarter leaf. The mixture of fresh yellow-greens and withering browns made it difficult to tell exactly what season it was.

As the trees closed in on us further, I lost myself in thoughts of the pilgrim site we had just visited. Reading "Jesus was here" on a rock got me thinking about how different the world was from 2,000 years earlier, when Christianity was born. If Jesus Christ walked the Earth today, He'd face completely different challenges in spreading the word. Scribbling his name on a rock or preaching on the side of a hill wouldn't do it, as He'd be forced to use modern technology to connect with people.

What would Jesus do? I wondered.

He would be lost without a website, so he'd secure the jesuschrist.com domain name. Then He'd collect email addresses on His homepage in exchange for free e-books (ghostwritten by Matthew, Mark, Luke and John). He'd invite people to get to know Him better through live on-line chat, and then be forced to subcontract temps in India to keep up with the demand. A natural people-person, Jesus would become a social networking guru. On Facebook, He'd friend complete strangers. And rather than recruiting only 12 disciples, He'd recruit his entire high-school graduating class. He'd be so into Twitter that the question "What would Jesus do?" would become redundant, as people would already know what He'd just been up to. After converting most of the planet, Jesus would sell jesuschrist.com to Google for $4.18 trillion and retire to Miami.

At the crest of the hill, I stopped and looked back over the oak woods, the altar, the meadow, dairy farm and second woods below, and the towns in the valley under that. It was beautiful, but the bright sun had melted away the early morning's mysteries and everything looked rather matter-of-fact. As I turned to face the view in the opposite direction and the city of Astorga about an hour's walk away, I thought to myself how I needed to clean the house, redo the upstairs bathroom and throw away some clothes when I got home. It was not the most profound thought of the Camino, but it seemed manageable at least. And there was nothing immediate to be done.

WE ARRIVED IN ASTORGA at five minutes after noon, just in time to miss the famous clock strike 12. The clouds were low and it looked like rain. But our spirits were high because, on this night, we would be staying at Hotel Gaudí (☆☆☆) in the *Plaza de Eduardo de Castro*.

"Antoni Gaudí designed Hotel Gaudí," said Rita, reading her guidebook.

"Really?" I said. "This is going to be amazing. I have always wanted to see one of his buildings."

"Well tonight you get to sleep in one," said Rita. "I suggest you wear your headlight to bed so you can click it on whenever you get an urge to stare at the ceiling."

As it started to rain, Rita referred to a map in her guidebook, led us down a narrow street to a large square, and delivered us to the front steps of Hotel Gaudí (☆☆☆).

"The hotel is remarkably square for Gaudí's work," I said to Rita and Fujiko, as we gazed up at its four-story brick facade. Fujiko held open the large glass French door, allowing Rita and me to enter first. Over the door, there was a window shaped like half of a wagon wheel.

"Interesting windows," I said.

Inside, and several steps down, we saw a fine dining room, panelled in what I imagined to be solid oak. Elderly women were enjoying lunch, chatting and sipping wine, dressed in their Sunday best.

Beyond the steps to the dining room, two long narrow tables lined one of the hallway walls. They were topped with bronze statues of miniature Greek gods wrestling in rustic settings. Opposite the tables, a marble staircase wound its way around an out-of-service elevator that was under renovation. One workman banged away inside, while another sat on a red metal toolbox.

"I don't think there would have been an elevator in Gaudí's day," I said. "I believe the elevator is new."

At reception, I asked the woman for three rooms with private baths and views of the *Plaza de Eduardo de Castro*, and we each received a key with an impressive wooden "G" attached to it.

"Gaudí would have designed everything," I said, taking a room key numbered 101. "He would have designed everything from the 'G' on these keys to the wooden shelves where they are stored, to the desk at reception, to the marble staircase."

Then, single file, Rita first, Fujiko last, me in the middle, we wound our way around the elevator, walking up the marble stairs to the *first* floor.

"The first floor is plainer than I would have expected for a Gaudí masterwork," I said. "He has practised restraint throughout on this project."

Rita and Fujiko stood beside me as I turned the key and opened the door to Room 101. Perhaps they were as eager as me to see what Gaudí had done with the rooms. The wood-panelled bedroom was a fine example of Spanish Canadiana, with pine furniture and wood panelling.

"Similar to what we have seen elsewhere," I said. "But there is an elegance to this place that sets it apart."

Rita and Fujiko looked around, opening closet doors, turning on bedside lamps.

"I wonder if Gaudí ever spent time in the Americas," I added.

After getting settled, Rita, Fujiko and I decided to have lunch in a smoky tapas bar, as the hotel's dining room seemed overpriced. After that, Fujiko went one way to buy stamps; I headed in another to find an internet café; and Rita went off in a third to buy bandages for her blisters.

WHEN I RETURNED to Hotel Gaudí, I heard Rita and Fujiko laughing, so I knocked on their door. They had opened the wooden shutters and were pointing at a building across the way.

"I read the guidebook wrong," exclaimed Rita. "Gaudí didn't design the hotel. He designed the Episcopal Palace across the plaza!"

They pointed over the fresh green canopy of plane trees at the far end of the square at an oddly misshapen building. It looked like an inflatable sandcastle that had lost half of its air.

"Gaudí would have designed everything including the 'G' on these keys," said Rita, making fun of what I had said earlier.

"The elevator is new," said Fujiko, mocking me too.

"He practised restraint throughout," added Rita.

"No, I mean yes," said Fujiko, laughing uproariously, while I played at being a good sport.

I had it coming to me, I thought to myself. Why act like a know-it-all when it's wiser to admit I know less than I'm pretending?

DAY THIRTEEN

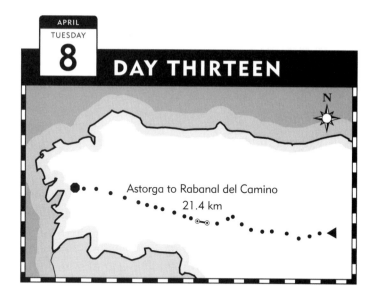

Astorga to Rabanal del Camino
21.4 km

THE NEXT MORNING, we met in Rita's room and had a picnic on the foot of her bed, eating mostly leftovers from the night before. For me, that meant an apple and half a head of broccoli. Rita ate dried toast*, cheese and almonds. Fujiko ate an orange and a pear and offered Rita and me individually wrapped granola bars from a box she had just opened.

"Today is Buddha's birthday," said Fujiko.

"Happy Birthday, Buddha," offered Rita.

"When was he born?" I asked.

"In 624 years B.C.," said Fujiko.

"That would make him over 2,000 years old if he were still sitting cross-legged under a tree," I said.

"His legs would be killing him," added Rita.

"Where was the Buddha born?" I asked.

"Lumbini," said Fujiko.

"Italy?"

89

---

* In Spain you buy dried toast in packages that you keep sealed so it doesn't get soggy.

"Nepal," corrected Fujiko. "His real name is Muni."

"Sounds like a cult."

"What does Muni mean?" asked Rita, ignoring what I had just said.

"Able One," said Fujiko.

So why did he just sit around all the time, I wondered?

Fujiko sat at the end of Rita's bed and told us the story of the Buddha.* When she was done, Rita asked, "You're a Buddhist, aren't you?"

"Yes, and I am also temporary Christian," said Fujiko, waving her pilgrim passport.

Then it was my turn: "The Buddha believed that every living creature had the same basic wish, to be happy and to avoid suffering."

"Yes?" said Fujiko, knowing there was more.

"Some pilgrims don't seem to want to avoid suffering. They seem to head out every morning looking for it. They certainly find it every night when they check into an *albergue* and sleep in a bunk or on a mat on the floor."

"Pain is unavoidable," said Fujiko.

"But I'm talking about suffering," I replied.

"Yes, Paul-*san*. When life become painful, it is not suffering until we think of it that way."

"The problem is in here," said Rita, tapping me playfully on the head.

SINGLE FILE, we followed the power lines out of town as they threaded through the foothills and over a range of mountains, basically tracing our path for the day. As it dawned on me that this day marked the midway point of our walk, I realized that I was going to be able to make it to Santiago quite easily. Oddly, the thought depressed me. The novelty, the mystery, the uncertainty were gone. Rather than feeling that I was challenging my limits, I was back to old questions like, "So, why am I doing this?"

---

* See Appendix H for an abridged version of *The Life of Buddha*, which I modified somewhat for a 21st century audience.

In the absence of an answer, I decided that maybe it was time to start trying to relax more. Other pilgrims didn't seem quite so obsessed with why they were here. On the surface at least, we were all the same: bound in Gore-Tex and walking to Santiago. Maybe I needed to just enjoy going through the motions. Maybe then I would loosen up, and if there was something inside I needed to know about, it would be able to rise to the surface and let me know it was there.

We entered the town of Murias de Rechivaldo along its southernmost stone-fenced border, stepping over puddles too muddy to see ourselves in. Just before the end of town, we opened a wooden door along an unmarked stucco wall and stopped to eat a second breakfast. Rita and I journaled as we ate, while Fujiko spoke to a tall brooding Finn in his early seventies.

"I have not taken a day off since I started two weeks ago," said the Finn. "I am walking 40 km a day."

"Aren't you tired? Why do you walk so far?" asked Fujiko.

"I lie in bed each night and I think of the other pilgrims passing me," said the Finn. "That keeps me walking the next day."

"Pilgrimage as rat race," Rita scribbled in her journal for only me to see. I wrote it, too.

Pilgrimage as rat race

Trying to keep up with pilgrims might work for the Finn, but he looked miserable. I've never been terribly competitive myself, and so I don't understand people who feel compelled to turn life into a competition, especially one that's impossible to win. If I were to turn the Camino into a race, I'd make the winner the person who finishes last. Or maybe, I'd make it a race where finishing was optional. It would certainly take some pressure off, if we were given a choice about how it ended.

BACK ON THE STREET, standing in the rain, we looked up at the mountains ahead, round clouds rolling across them. The sun shone through breaks in the clouds to momentarily transform this submerged world into a glittering oasis. In one such sun-blessed spot, three spinning wind turbines in a line were cast golden. On our left, across the valley, a rainbow rose from steely cliffs and arched steeply upward before stopping cold, halfway toward us and just below the grey underside of this turbulent sea-like sky.

As we climbed into the ever-changing mountains it occurred to me how it was nothing like walking across the uniform plains of the Meseta, where the scenery seemed as constant and still as stars on a clear and quiet night. Here, the land was shifting constantly. I turned along a ridge to face a new vista, and it revealed a completely different world and an array of mountains higher and more fearsome than I could have imagined. Step by step the world was changing. Step by rising step the seasons were rolling backward and leaves were seemingly being retracted into cold branches – until the trees were no longer in bud.

We continued our climb until just before noon, when we began seeing short old people wandering on the trail. I was always happy to see them because, on the Camino, short old people signalled a nearby town the way gulls at sea signal landfall.

"Land Ho," I cried out to Fujiko and Rita, who were waiting for me 100 metres ahead.

"Yee-haw!" shouted Fujiko back and Rita joined in with a "Howdy pardner."

As I caught up with the two women, they were do-si-do-ing on the edge of the small mountain town of El Ganso. There, wedged in a fork in the road, was either a mirage or a place called COWBOY BAR.

"Do you think it's a gay bar?" I asked Rita.

"For your sake, I hope not," said Rita, pointing at my waterproof Quasimodo costume. "You aren't exactly dressed for it, you know."

COWBOY BAR was housed in a simple A-frame cottage. Its expansive raftered ceiling was like an inverted whaling ship covered in white paint. Hanging from the rafters, nailed to the walls, and scattered about rustic tabletops hewn from giant trees was an impressive collection of authentic North American cowboy paraphernalia. We looked around, taking in everything from wagon wheels to rusted pitchforks, from cowboy hats to cowboy boots, from metal lanterns to gold-pans, from racks of antelope antlers to wooden harnesses once shouldered by mighty oxen. A sign from the '50s hung next to a mullioned window on the right, which struck me as exceptionally gay. It read: "COWBOYS, LEAVE YOUR GUNS AT THE BAR."

A tall, thin bartender smiled at us. Behind him, strings of thick sausage hung from the rafters.

«*Hola* Cowboy», said Fujiko.

«*La la la la, la la la*», said the bartender in return, as he leaned over to kiss each of us on both cheeks.

"How gay is that?" I asked Rita.

"Don't be silly, he's just Spanish," she answered.

"Maybe," I answered. "But I am turning on my gaydar just in case."

As the bartender served us sausage and repeated shots of vodka, I completed a chart in my notebook to decide whether he was gay or just Spanish.

Behaviour	Gay	Just Spanish
Kisses me before he knows my name	✓	✓
Dresses like a cowboy but doesn't own a cow.	✓	
Nice / Clean / Well-dressed / In shape	✓	✓
Laughs a lot / Über-flamboyant	✓	✓
Hangs out in a bar all day	✓	✓
Sausage plays key role in life	✓	✓
Has cousins in Nebraska		✓

As we prepared to leave, the bartender sent us on our way with two-cheek kisses and a collegial pat on my back. "He's just Spanish," insisted Rita.

THE REST OF THE CLIMB was marked by an overwhelming vodka-induced need to pee, which I did repeatedly behind trees, which got smaller and smaller the higher we climbed, until I was whizzing behind a bush that barely hid what I was up to. The scenery didn't seem nearly as scenic as this morning's; I didn't see a single "glittering oasis" nor "one such sun-blessed spot." The wind turbines were still spinning, though. Then again, so was everything else. In the late afternoon light, everything – the grass, the stone walls, the trees and the rocks – turned yellowish-green, which I found slightly nauseating. Shortly after passing an elderly green man walking his green billy goat, we arrived at Rabanal del Camino, and we were soon standing on the steps of *Refugio Gaulcemo*, which Rita said was run by the Confraternity of St. James in London.*

During a supper of leftovers from our packs, the British women running the *refugio* played doctor to a Spanish pilgrim named Heraclio, who had become legendary over the last few days because of an infected big toe (on the right foot). His determination to continue in the face of suffering had been the talk among pilgrims for the previous three days. It was pretty cool to meet him face to face, so I opened my notebook to PAUL'S INCOMPLETE GUIDE TO PILGRIM SPANISH, pointed to his infected toe which now looked like a reused tea bag and read aloud concernedly, leaving out any suggestion of amputation.

«El aspecto de su dedo gordo del pie no es bueno. ¿Puedo ayudarle?»

("Your big toe looks really bad. Can I help you?")

He smiled dimly, and I felt vindicated for having taken a day to write PAUL'S INCOMPLETE GUIDE TO PILGRIM SPANISH. Instead of being complete strangers, whose differences (including language) outnumbered commonalities four million to one, Hercalio and I were fellow pilgrims sharing the same path.

As I pondered, the British women attended to him by pouring hot pots of water into a plastic bin where he was soaking his

---

* They call it a *refugio*, but it's just another *albergue*. The Brits always have to say things their own way, eh?

toe, as if they were making repeated pots of tea. I felt badly that Rita wasn't getting the same attention. Surely, her feet were as bad as his. But I guess they were not technically infected. She was suffering, poor dear – just not quite enough.

DAY FOURTEEN

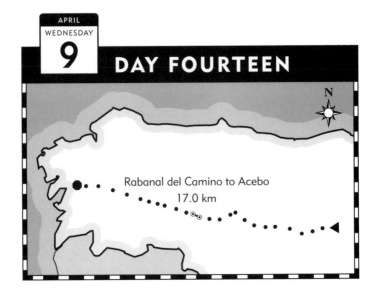

Rabanal del Camino to Acebo
17.0 km

N

IF GOD CREATED HEAVEN AND EARTH in seven days, I think He did a pretty good job. But personally, I would have done a few things differently. For one, I would have lightened up on gravity a little so mountains were easier to climb. I would have even gone so far as to make the law of gravity optional, at least for pilgrims like us who were about to climb to the highest point of the entire Camino, atop the mighty Mount Irago.

According to Rita's guidebook, it was 1,505 metres high, but it seemed illusively higher. Every time we turned a corner, I expected to see the summit – but I never did! It was as though someone was inflating unseen parts of the mountain as we climbed, so it got taller and taller the higher we went. Snow lay in patches around our feet, reminiscent of the train ride from Madrid to Burgos two weeks earlier. The main difference was that we were climbing on our own steam, unprotected from the cold. Yet I was warm, having improvised another winter coat out of a rain jacket stuffed with a sleeping bag.

On the way up, we stopped to pay our respects at the ruins of a church. Its empty bell tower was the only thing that rose out of its crumbled foundation and its arrant silence haunted the landscape.

Where is the voice of God now? I wondered.

And as I contemplated the church's silent remains, my mind wandered back in time to the last time God spoke to me. It was November of 1993, the opening night of a community theatre production of the musical *Oliver!* and I was playing Mr. Sowerberry – a seven-minute part near the top of Act 1. At the last minute, the director decided that I'd carry two huge bouquets of gladioli, which meant I couldn't see where I was going. In the midst of a sea of laughter, conjured by my own antics – and the image of two skinny legs animating two pots of flowers – I heard God's James-Earl-Jones-like voice inside my head saying emphatically, YOU – ARE – BRILLIANT!

It felt like a spiritual moment, as yet unmatched in my life. In that instant, I knew I was to be the great actor I had dreamed of becoming. And it might have come to pass had I not, with my very next step, fallen off the stage and disappeared into the blackness of the orchestra pit, gladioli flying every which way. This was more than a fall. This was the moment in my life when I realized that the voice inside my head was not God, but a role I had assumed myself.

"Oh God, you have to step back into the light," said the voice inside my head, with less conviction than before.

"Whatever you do, it had better be Shakespearean," it added.

And so, when I climbed back up on stage with the few blooms I could gather, I did so with aplomb – a performance worthy of Laurence Olivier, Sean Penn, and Robin Williams all rolled into one. As a result, more than half of the audience was fooled into believing it was part of the show, and I played the rest of the scene without any shame or embarrassment.

Looking back though, I felt humbled to have thought that God was there with me, inside my own head, walking me through a minor role in a community theatre performance. If God exists, I thought to myself, He surely has better things to do than to help amateurs like me get the laughs I so badly crave.

Since then, I no longer believe that God cares so much what I'm up to on or off stage. If the Creator of the Universe exists, He surely has better things to do than stroke my ego. I have come to learn that I'm pretty much on my own in that department.

Beyond the church tower were fields dappled with shadow and light. Above, steely clouds floated by ominously like the hulls of heavy ships. Through patches of blue, sheaths of golden sun appeared like oars stroking the air and moving the boats past. Where we stood, the landscape was silver from all the light that reflected off wet grey stones.

At 10:43 a.m., we did actually arrive at the top of the mountain, just as a German couple was cycling down the other side at breakneck speed. A modest iron cross atop a giant pole marked the highest point. The monument rose from a pile of rocks that pilgrims had left behind as part of an age-old Camino tradition. Apparently, we were meant to leave a stone from home as a way of symbolizing some grief or anger we've chosen to leave behind. Not knowing what else to do, I stared meaningfully at a heap of other people's stones that represented abandoned personal baggage that didn't belong to me.

"We made it," said Rita. "It took us 14 days to do it, but we made it to the top."

She climbed over the rocks until she reached the foot of the iron cross. There, she knelt down, reached into her pack and removed a tiny pebble.

"My dad gave this to me. It's from my parents' garden in Aurora," she said.

Fujiko dug through her own pack for something to leave behind. As she removed her angel card, she said, "I pray for Amiko-*san*."

We bowed our heads and I remembered our friend Amiko-*san*, who had intended to be with us. She had defied gravity with laughter but succumbed in the end to cancer.

Fujiko wedged her angel card between two rocks and said, "Amiko-*san*, I give you angel card." Then she read the card one last time. "Transformation."

AS IT STARTED TO SNOW AGAIN and the rocks reflected the day's grey light, we pulled out our ponchos and put them on, making sure our backpacks were also covered. We clambered down the side of the mountain like the back ends of vaudevillian asses missing their fronts. We traced an ancient twisting goat path that threaded its way through grey meadows, all the way down to the rooftops of Acebo. As we arrived in town, we came across a man on the main street, outside a barn. He was wearing a burgundy scarf and held a large black umbrella. He was giving off an odd vibe – as though he might have been a Buddhist used car salesman.

"Hello, are you spending the night?" he asked.

"We hope to," said Rita.

"I own a bed and breakfast. Please follow me," he said, and told us that his name was Santiago: "Just like the saint."*

Just then, the barn door behind him slid open and a brown cow (with the dreamiest brown eyes) nudged her way onto the street. She looked somehow human, as if she was wearing red lipstick and false eyelashes. She toddled onto the street as if she had been eating alfalfa spiked with sherry. When she noticed us, she paused and then looked at Santiago with utter bafflement. It was as if she was saying, "You never told me we had company."

"This is Ruby," said Santiago, smiling at us. "She thinks she is my wife. She has been with me since she was born – it is a long story."

Ruby pushed past. And Santiago followed her in the same dogged way Helmut had followed Dolores. Intrigued, we waited until Santiago returned several minutes later.

"Ruby is a handful," he said as he led us in the opposite direction.

We followed Santiago to the edge of the mountain, past a well-tended Japanese garden and into his beige stuccoed home. Two mutts greeted us with the uncultured exuberance of hillbillies, while a black cat stared us down from the back of a reclining chair that sat by the fire.

"Please make yourselves at home," said Santiago, pointing to a round dining room table as he disappeared into the kitchen.

----

* In Spanish, James translates to three different names: Santiago, Diego and Jaime. Shouldn't they have to settle on one?

Santiago's dogs, quarantined by their master on the Persian carpet in front of the fire, were looking at us amicably, dripping friendly slobber meant for us. The black cat luxuriated in the fire's heat and wanted to be left alone to lie quietly in languor.

Santiago went back and forth from the kitchen to the dining room, serving us lentil soup with olive oil and freshly ground sesame, followed by an earthy vegetable stew with sticky white rice. For dessert, he offered bread pudding, fresh strawberries, and an organic cookie that had *"eco – bio"* stamped on it. All the while, he filled and refilled our glasses with red wine until he decided, too late, that we'd had enough.

By the time we finished eating, we did not want to leave, so I took a private room for €40 that faced the snow-capped mountains. The €40 included a bed, dinner and breakfast. Fujiko and Rita chose to bunk like sisters in a room with single beds, for half of what I paid.

"This is your house now," said Santiago, counting our money at the dining room table.

«*Gracias. Es muy amable*», I said. ("Thank you. It is very kind.")

Our house was warm and tranquil with a distinct Zen feeling to it. It was uncluttered with the exception of a sitting army of jade Buddhas, arranged willy-nilly throughout, and a tangle of wind chimes dangling overhead. Inexpensive yet stylish furniture gave off a quiet calm by not trying to be more than it was.

"FOR THE FIRST TIME ON THE CAMINO, I feel like I am on vacation," I said to Rita and Fujiko. "How about a walk into town?"

After a quick tour of the main street, corner grocery (closed), post office (also closed), we discovered the only thing to do in this sleepy window-boxed town was drink. So in the bar, seated under two television sets, one playing soccer, the other forecasting rain for days, Rita and I downed a draught of beer and a bag of potato chips each, while Fujiko sipped on green tea.

"May we join you?" asked a bellowing voice, as its linebacker-sized frame blocked any escape.

"My name is Rob. I'm American. This is my wife Alexandra. She's from the Philippines."

Rob was the first American we had met on the Camino. There had been plenty of Canadians – enough to support several Tim Hortons, in fact.* But there had been a marked absence of our neighbours to the south.

"How long have you been married?" asked Rita, pleasantly.

"Six months," said Rob. "I was married before."

"Three times," added Alexandra.

"The first time I walked the Camino, I walked 25 miles a day," offered Rob.

"That's a lot," said Rita.

"And I carried 65 pounds on my back."

"That's more than half what I weigh," said Alexandra.

"It was July and very busy," continued Rob. "Sometimes, I had to walk an extra 12 miles before I found a floor to sleep on."

"How far are you walking tomorrow?" asked Rita.

"Not so far," said Rob. "Alexandra is not much of a walker."

"We live in LA," explained Alexandra. "I drive everywhere."

I couldn't help but wonder if the two of them would make it to Santiago together, or if God had a woman with more stamina waiting for Rob in Ponferrada.

"I bought $4,000 worth of gear so we could walk as far as possible," said Rob. "But I have my cell phone in case it gets to be too much."

"We'll call our driver if we need him to drive us partway," explained Alexandra.

For our first American pilgrim, Rob was living up to all of the US stereotypes. He seemed to be walking the Camino to make the American Dream come true. He was as driven as the Finn we met yesterday, but he was full of good old American optimism. And he had it all: a trophy wife, a driver and cash to spare. He seemed less on a pilgrimage than a victory parade. I was trying hard not to judge him too harshly.

"Why are you walking the Camino again?" asked Rita.

---

* For the non-Canadian reader, Tim Hortons is the McDonald's of Canadian donut shops: over 75 trillion served, or something like that.

"I wanted Alexandra to see it," said Rob. "I walked the Camino 15 years ago to get myself focused so I could go into business."

Again, I was struck by the gap between Rob's ambition and the deeper reasons why many people walk the Camino. It all seemed so shallow to me. But then, I thought about myself. Who was I fooling? It was not as though I was walking to cure cancer. And who was I to judge him anyway? I'm in business too. And, just like him, I had my own creature comforts on the Camino, such as hotels instead of hostels. Why was I judging Rob so harshly? It was a good question. As Rob continued talking to Rita, I pretended to watch the weather on TV.

As I did, I decided that I, too, was shallow. I had been away from an audience while on the Camino, and I realized that life never feels more real than when I'm on stage. If I don't have an audience for extended periods, I start to feel vulnerable. Without the heady rush of performance, it's not as easy for me to be convinced that life has any particular meaning.

Shouldn't I do more? Maybe. But what? Hopefully the world needs shallow people like me, I thought to myself. Hopefully the world needs people like me to skim the surface in search of laughs and to keep things light, because it's what I'm drawn to – what I know – what I do. It's my calling, whether people are listening or not. And Rob, obviously, has a calling of his own – one for which he's particularly driven.

I decided to cut Rob some slack. It's not like there's a rulebook written about the Camino. He was free to make of it whatever he chose because it was his journey and not mine.

"We'd love people to walk with," said Rob ominously. "Maybe we'll see you tomorrow."

WHEN WE RETURNED "HOME", Santiago was waiting for us with a spinach and broccolini salad, tangy San Simón cheese and buttered toast, along with a bottle of red wine (which we didn't drink).

«*Buen apetito*», said Santiago. And then, as he headed out into the black night, followed by his dogs, he added, "I must now find Ruby."

About an hour later, as I lay awake watching the faint glow of moonlight on the mountains through the window, I heard, coming from downstairs, the clattering of the storm door's glass, as Santiago's dogs wildly pushed open the door. Santiago's tired voice admonished their exuberance and then softly said words only he and the Buddhas were supposed to hear, "Ruby, whatever was I thinking when I rescued you?"

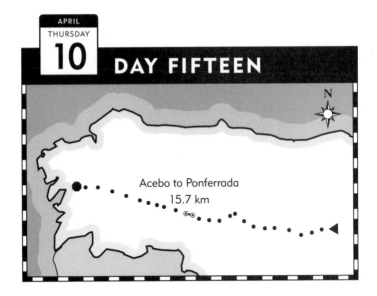

Acebo to Ponferrada
15.7 km

I SAT AGAINST CAREFULLY FLUFFED PILLOWS at the head of the bed, and looked out the window at mountains, framed by white lace curtains. This is paradise, I thought to myself. But soon a thick fog swallowed the mountains whole, and the white lace curtains framing the windows all but merged with the grey of another day.

Downstairs, Santiago waited for us next to the fire, with the black cat on his lap. The cat leaped from its warm berth, casting a sideways glance at us as Santiago stood to say good-bye. One at a time, he held our hands in his, looked at us deeply with the dark smiling eyes of a living saint, said something incomprehensible that sounded really nice and then gave each of us a two-cheek kiss. Each in turn, we smiled and giggled nervously.

«*Buen Camino*», said Santiago, before holding the door open.

We stepped outside, filed through the Japanese garden and past the barking dogs, walked up the lane and headed toward the town. The sun was up but the fog made everything as opaque as milk.

At the bottom end of town, we met up with Rob and Alexandra. She was the best, most expensively dressed Little Bo Peep I had ever seen. She even had a pilgrim staff that was curled at one end. If a flock of sheep would have helped her walk further, I'm sure that Rob would have rented one. It was hard not to laugh, let alone not judge.

We greeted each other, and I smiled from ear to ear to keep from giggling. Then we headed out of town together, until we reached the first major road at the bottom of a steep decline. There, Rob played tour guide.

"This is a memorial to a German cyclist who died here in 1987," said Rob.

Oh, I thought to myself, as I suddenly changed the tone of my inner voice, this is not something to mock. We stood in silence, looking up at the sculpture of a riderless bicycle popping a wheelie.

Though it was meant to remember a death, it was full of life. The bicycle floated, careened or soared ... it was hard to tell which, and so I stared, imagining the life that was lost in inspiring this statue. Was he young? Brave? Daring? Foolish? Did he believe? What were his last thoughts? Had he accomplished what he'd hoped for? We stood for a few more moments of silence until Rob moved on, followed by Little Bo Peep and then us.

As I walked, I reflected on the deceased pilgrim, and started to feel the sadness of life and its uninvited end. As we walked under a canopy of white peach blossoms camouflaged against the grey, I wondered if it was raining when the German pilgrim lost his life. As we waded through water rushing over loose mountain pebbles on the slippery rivulet of a path, I thought of the frailty of life and started to tear up a little. As we passed yellow primroses scattered at the feet of three leafless twisted oaks, I imagined my own inevitable end. But as we descended through a verdant ridge, and the first Spanish broom plants bloomed white like exploding fireworks, my mood brightened and I cried instead at the joy of being alive. And when we walked through anemic mountain peonies I cried at the countless examples of grace in my life, including grandma Grace, who had just passed away.

It's the most broodingly beautiful day of the Camino so far, I thought to myself. And with that, in the privacy of my own rain hood, I cried a little more.*

I felt a need to go home.

SHORTLY AFTER STEPPING OFF the mountain onto another fertile plain, we walked past a boarded-up church, followed a medieval bridge across the raging Río Meruelo and entered the narrow streets of the picturesque but deserted town of Molinaseca. We wondered where we might eat until we passed a plate glass window and, appearing to be stuffed in there like the fad from the '50s that tried to get as many as possible into a phone booth, we saw a crush of pilgrims. It turned out to be a tiny bar. Outside, a limousine was waiting. We added our stuff to the pile of gear blocking the entranceway and morphed with the huddle inside.

Everyone who had been averaging 20 km a day was shoulder to shoulder: a happy Dolores and an exhausted Helmut; Hercalio, the Spanish guy with the toe (and boyfriend Fabían, too); the Austrian girls (bussing it most of the way); a group of five Germans we had not seen since Burgos; Rob, Little Bo Peep, a cast of lesser characters and the three of us.

A woman behind a minuscule bar was making bite-sized sandwiches to order. We each asked for something and were surprised but pleased with what we got instead. Then we squeezed through the crowd, looking for a free table.

"Having fun yet?" I asked Helmut.

"How is your toe?" I asked the Spanish guy, accidentally bumping it as I passed.

"You walk the whole way?" asked the Austrian girls incredulously.

---

* Before you judge me too harshly you should know that everybody cries on the Camino. Everybody cries, has a temper tantrum and experiences at least one moment of elation beyond human understanding. And they apparently happen when you least expect them to. At least that's what I've been told... One down, two to go.

"We thought we might since it *is* a pilgrimage," I replied.

"You're grumpy," said Rita.

"Very glumpy!"* added Fujiko.

"Sorry... I'm just tired of being on the move all the time. Last night I finally found a place that felt normal to me. It was quiet, comfortable and aesthetic. But, today, we're moving again and I'm tired. I don't know if I have it in me to keep talking sweetly to pilgrims I might never see again.

"And as for Spain, it's getting me down. Everything is off in Spain and I have to constantly tilt my head to make it feel normal. Phone cards in a hardware store? Who thought that one up? In Canada, you'd buy them in convenience stores because they're convenient. But then, when you're up partying 24 hours a day like the Spanish, who needs convenience? You can just pick it up between dinner, drinking, smoking, partying or napping. There are so many in-betweens in the Spanish lifestyle that convenience would be wasted on them."

As I spoke, my voice got louder. I couldn't help but sense the pilgrims at neighbouring tables might have been listening. It was a heightened sensitivity I had that gauges an audience's interest, but that I sometimes forget to turn off in social situations.

"And the supermarkets ... don't get me started on the supermarkets. Heaven forbid you touch a piece of fruit with your bare hands. The grocer will react as though you reached down and fondled his own."

Dolores and Helmut at the next table guffawed.

"They *are* listening," I thought to myself, and so I heightened my delivery slightly:

"You'd be arrested for public naughtiness when all you did was grab a banana."

Dolores and Helmut laughed again. Behind them, Rob glanced up to see what was going on.

----

* The Japanese have a hard time distinguishing between the letters "R" and "L". They only have one sound for both, and it's somewhere in between the two. I don't want to make fun of them, but it *is* funny. To the Japanese, "grumpy" and "*glumpy*" are exactly the same word, as are "*peregrino*" and "*pellegrino*".

"How am I supposed to know how it all works if nobody tells me?" I asked. "How am I supposed to know those plastic gloves aren't for surgery – but for fondling fruit?"

"Unless the guy's behind the counter," exclaimed Rob. "Then you have to ask him to fondle your fruit for you."

"Exactly," I responded. "But how am I supposed to know what to ask for?"

"Fake it until you make it!" cried Rob.

"Right again! I mean, who's to know that squash in Spanish is *una cucurbitácea.*"

«*¿Una cucurbitácea?*» asked the Spanish guy with the toe.

"Back home, we don't have the time of day to say *una cucurbitácea* when what we want is squash," I explained, not sure the Spanish guy understood or not. But he was smiling, so I didn't really care. The entire bar had suddenly come alive and I was aware of laughter throughout.

"*Vat* about *ze* timers on *ze* toilets?" asked Helmut. "Have you ever seen *anyssing* like *zeez* toilets?"

"No, Helmut, I can't say that I have. Not even in Germany is that part of the human condition so measured. Who, other than an engineer addicted to fibre would decide that we would get 45 seconds (no more and no less) before it's 'lights out' when we're sitting on the can? I don't know how many times I sat there enjoying a little needed relief when suddenly it's like 'click' and the lights switch off."

"And *zer* are no *vindows eizzer*," offered Helmut.

"Exactly! There are no windows because that would be too *convenient.*"

Helmut, in particular, was shining brighter than I had seen. It was as though the laughing had fooled him into thinking his day's walk was done, or not quite as daunting as it was a few minutes earlier.

"You're killing me," said a little voice inside my head, and I certainly felt I was on a roll. But rather than take over the bar and slip into stand-up, I decided to lower my voice again. As much as I loved the feeling of people laughing at their stress and letting go of it, I decided to rant more privately to my own walking mates. Besides, the bar had been ignited with foreign chatter in comedic tones. As sacred as the Camino is to many, I was relieved to have found room to voice some respectful irreverence.

"And then there's the whole lisp thing," I continued so only Rita and Fujiko could hear. "I mean, I had a speech impediment when I was a kid so I know what it's like.* If only the Spanish would admit to having a problem, they could pronounce the letter 's' with just enough 'th-th-th-th' to sound like they've sprung a leak, without suggesting their manhood's been removed.

"There are other Spanish countries like Mexico where they've outgrown the lisp – why are they holding onto it in Spain? Does their love for all things Spanish include an unbridled passion for sounding effeminate? Do they think they *thound fanthier* than the *retht* of *uth*? Spain could, if Spain wanted to, be more like us. They could meet us halfway. All they'd have to do is give up some of the things I find challenging about them, while keeping the things I love most, like cheese sandwiches on bread so fresh that you forget there's nothing in the sandwich except bread and cheese..."

"Are you finished?" asked Rita.

"Well, then there's the Museum of Ham in Astorga," I continued. "I mean what kind of civilization evolves to the point that they open a museum dedicated to ham and place it in a major square? Don't get me started," I said. "Don't get me started."

Fujiko didn't know what to say, but smiled rather politely. It's not a very Japanese thing to rant like this in public. In fact, a Japanese rant would last a sentence and a half and would contain the clause, "You have accomplished so much, you must be very tired..." Rita didn't seem like she knew what to say, either, though she'd heard me rant before. After all, the three of us climbed Mount Fuji together, and we had been sidelined for

---

* I was pulled out of class in grade six for my inability to pronounce the letter "R". I remember my mother and grandmother standing by the stove watching me as I did my homework on the kitchen table: "He has difficulty pronouncing his 'R's," said my mother, to which my grandmother pursed her lips and shook her head concernedly.

24 hours by rain, sitting in a hut at 11,500 ft. There had been 100 people in that hut when the monsoon struck and we had no running water, no showers and no windows. As sweet as humanity is and as proud as I am to be a part of the species that invented religion and fire and heaven and hell, humanity can create a lot of stink in a sealed box at 11,500 feet over a 24-hour period. And one man can surely learn how to rant.

Back at the Camino, Rita just smiled and said nothing. So I harrumphed and left it at that. And I decided to behave.

After lunch, we left the bar on foot, heading back into the rain as the Austrian girls climbed into the back seat of Rob and Alexandra's limousine. Barely seeing them through the tinted glass, I smiled and waved dumbly at my own reflection. As the limo pulled away, we stepped onto yet another unfriendly highway.

"What would we have lost by taking a ride?" I asked Rita.

"Our self-respect," she countered.

"Is that all?" I asked. "And why is it so important to walk the whole way?"

"So we can say we did."

"Who needs to walk the whole way to say they did?" I asked, but neither Rita nor Fujiko responded.

Rita chose the scenic route, which wound its way through drenched fields and then meandered into Ponferrada through another dismal industrial wasteland, adding an extra 55 minutes to the day's ordeal.

As we arrived in the city, I passed a young Korean who had obviously lost his group.

«Buen Camino», I said, smiling as I walked past, knowing that Fujiko and Rita would stop to help him out (which they did, adding yet another 15 minutes to the day.)

In front of the medieval castle in the centre of the old city, I surveyed three locals on how best to get to Hotel Madrid (☆☆☆), only to be reminded how divergent local opinions could be. Following what I thought to be the best of each of their directions, I led us through the old town and snaked back and forth across the river for another 45 minutes until, at 1:35, we finally arrived at Hotel Madrid (☆☆☆), where we muddied the red carpet.

THAT EVENING, Fujiko and Rita suggested we attend Mass at the famous 16th century basilica. I would rather have slept, but agreed to go so as not to be alone. I must have been too tired for religion because I was not as well-behaved as the women would have liked. In fact, I couldn't stop giggling at the priest's Castillian lisp, which was the gayest I'd heard.

During one bit of laughter, Rita jabbed me with her elbow, and I was reminded of the last time I had as much fun in church. It was 40 years earlier and I was seated in between an older brother and sister. We were playing with a yellow plastic Hercules ring. In spite of being told to be quiet, we carried on until the Mass ended. When we returned home, my father called us into the living room and lectured us on obedience.

He asked my older sister: "Will you do it again?"

"No," she replied.

Then he asked my older brother: "Will you do it again?"

"No," he replied.

Then he asked me: "Will you do it again?"

At that moment, I felt such affection for my father. He seemed reasonable and loving in spite of his authority. Maybe that's what gave me the courage to say what I said next. The word "No" would have been the easier, more sensible answer. But I was only three, awash in my father's disciplinary love, and I wanted to know what happened if you answered "Yes."

I smiled boldly and looked into my father's eyes. "Yes," I said, understanding neither the question nor the answer.

With that, my father pulled down my pants and spanked my bottom, after which I ran confusedly into my mother's arms. It was very discombobulating to say the least. As my world spun and my bottom burned I learned that "Yes" could be a dangerous word. Forty years later, I wondered if I still lacked the courage to use it.

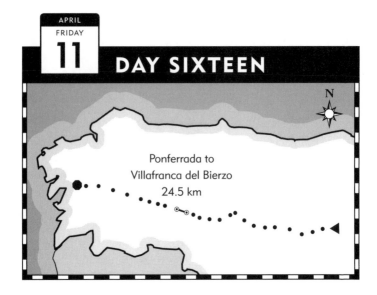

DAY SIXTEEN

Ponferrada to
Villafranca del Bierzo
24.5 km

N

"**IF YOU EVER WANT TO CREATE HAVOC** in northern Spain, arrive with a bucket of yellow paint and draw arrows pointing any which way," I said to Rita, as we stepped out of the front doors of Hotel Madrid (☆☆☆), a decidedly new bounce in my step. "Pilgrims depend on the yellow arrows to find their way. Point them in the wrong direction and they will become hopelessly lost," I added mischievously.

We then proceeded to scour downtown Ponferrada for yellow arrows pointing toward Santiago.

"You've jinxed us," said Rita about 15 minutes later.

"That's ridiculous," I replied. "At least if somebody had painted arrows in the *wrong* direction, we would be going *somewhere*."

"I find shell," called Fujiko from across the street, and our 24.5-km day began.

As we walked up a treed boulevard toward the northern edge of town, I glanced back at the mountains we had scaled the day before. Below fluffy clouds that cut off the peaks, alpine meadows shone with breathtaking greens and golds. Rita and

Fujiko snapped photos, as did other pilgrims who thought to stop and look back to enjoy the view of what we'd hiked.

At this lower elevation, the climate seemed more temperate. Spring had returned, and roses and lilacs were in full bloom. In fact, cabbages survived the winter here and gardens boasted heads resting on twisted stalks three feet high. They replenished themselves as soup-making housewives removed just the outer leaves as needed. Fujiko called them cabbage trees. A woman sitting on a salvaged car seat on the far side of a cabbage grove waved at us. *«Buen Camino»*, she cried.

A giant stork floated overhead and landed in a huge nest over the town hall of the village we entered. It was as if the quaint building had a crown. As I watched, I thought to myself how there was a sense of optimism in the air that we had not felt in days. And then it rained again.

But in spite of the rain it was a pleasant day, even if I couldn't admit it to anyone but myself. It was cool, thank goodness, which was good. With all the impermeable gear I was wearing, I could have easily been trapped in a walking sauna.

As we walked, I zipped and unzipped the many openings of my raincoat and pants, like a tall ship adjusting its sails in changing winds. I opened the zippers under my arms to let in a cool breeze where it was needed most. I unzipped my rain pants by the ankles to chill down my overheating legs. When the wind picked up, I removed the poncho because I was warm enough and my backpack had its own waterproof cover. I continued with this changing tack until we stopped for lunch in the oddly named town of Cacabelos,* and Rita led us to a restaurant mentioned in her guidebook.

"This is food heaven," she promised, standing under a sign that read *El Apóstol*. We entered a fashionable crypt-like space where the sound system was playing *Lo Mejor del Soul* (The Best of Soul). The air was cool, a nice contrast to the humidity outside that was getting downright steamy.

A handsome waiter with grey temples greeted us at the bottom of the stone steps leading to the dining room. We were

----

* If you studied Latin and like bathroom humour, Cacabelos is a funny name.

seated at a table that had a white linen tablecloth and napkins. He lit three white candles, handed us menus and disappeared. He returned moments later with a carafe of tap water and two others of red and white wine.

"Women have taught me to speak Italian, German and French, but not English ... *yet*," he said looking across the table at Rita. He paused momentarily and then returned to the kitchen.

"Rita has new boyfriend," said Fujiko, peering over her menu.

"Stop it," said Rita. "He *is* attractive though."

"Do you like him?" I asked.

"Keep walking," said Fujiko emphatically.

Lunch was lentil soup and a groaning platter of chicken legs (both inescapable on the Camino) and a giant salad bowl full of fries. For dessert, Fujiko and I had cheesecake, made with farm-fresh cheese. Even though it smelled like hay, it tasted divine.

"The saltiness of real Spanish cheese," I said to the waiter, who looked at me unimpressed.

«*¡Delicioso!*» said Fujiko to the waiter, whose eyes were fixed on Rita.

"Your ice cream cake, madam," he said as he placed a thick slice of nirvana before her.

"No plastic tub?" asked Rita.

"Is it okay, madam?" asked the waiter worriedly.

"Yes. Oh, yes," Rita assured him. "It's just that at every restaurant where we have eaten, they have served us ice cream in plastic tubs, like the ones you'd find in a store."

"Not here," said the waiter softly. "We serve you only the best."

"Is it getting hot in here or is it just me?" I asked, as I stood up and pulled my outer rain pants down to my ankles so I could cool off a little, before quickly sitting again. It was a fancy place and I was pleased that the table of old-lady locals next to us hardly looked up from their own chicken legs to see what I had just done.

"Classy," said Rita.

"It's okay," I answered back, placing my napkin on my lap. "I still have my hiking pants on underneath. At least now I won't be so warm."

The waiter, who saw what I had just done, said something huffy in Spanish ending in "*encia*" and left.

Rita, Fujiko and I sat and chatted for 30 minutes as the waiter returned to refill pots of tea and carafes of wine.

"We are free spirits," I said to them. "Happy to drift through Spain forever."

"But I will be happy to get back to my life at home," said Rita.

"Me, too," said Fujiko. "It is cherry blossom time in Japan."

We split the bill in three and Rita took it up to the counter to pay. I pulled up my rain pants, nodding obligingly at the old ladies next to us.

Back on the street, the clouds had cleared and the day had been handed over to the hot sun.

"What now?" I asked.

"Maybe we should visit the town," said Rita.

"Yes, better to digest," agreed Fujiko, patting her tummy.

As the women consulted their guidebooks for sights to see, I dropped my outer rain pants to my ankles again. I placed my hands on my hips, feeling rather clever for staying cool in this heat.

Suddenly the waiter reappeared. «A-a-a-ah, *Señorina, Señora ... Señor*», he said. "I sorry, but napkin is missing."

"We certainly did not take one." I replied.

"What is that?" asked Rita, pointing between my ankles. Fujiko put her hand to her mouth.

"I think we found your napkin," said Rita to the waiter.

I looked down. Between my ankles, wedged in the seat of my rain pants, was a white table napkin, with bits of cheese-cake still on it. I likely never removed it from my lap before pulling up my rain pants.

"Sorry," said Rita to the waiter, rolling her eyes. She then broke into laughter. Fujiko tried but failed to contain herself for my sake.

I was not sure what to do first; reach down and return the napkin to the waiter or waddle over to Rita and get her to shut up. I shuffled towards Rita like a legless chicken wobbling on its hips. I was not sure how I'd shush her, but I knew I had to reach her quickly or this scene was going to get even more embarrassing.

After three toddles, I lost my balance and fell sideways toward the waiter who had no choice but to catch me or let me fall to the ground. The old ladies emerged from the restaurant as a group of smoking old men stepped out of the bar opposite. Both groups were curious to learn how I ended up in the waiter's arms with my rain pants around my ankles.

«¡Mire!» cried the old ladies, breaking out in laughter.

They darted across the street without looking, and brought a Santana Motors 1.9L *Stella* to a screeching halt. A clenched fist appeared out of the driver's side. Then they corralled their men on the far side of the street, giddy as pre-teens.

«¡Mire: tiene un pañal para adulto en sus pantalones!» said one, as she pointed at the napkin lodged in my rain pants.

"What did she say?" asked Rita.

"Something about adult incontinence diapers," I replied, casting aside my pride.

"She is the ringleader," I added. "If there is going to be any peace in Cacabelos, she is going to have to go first."

The waiter stood me up and took a step back. He held his hand out, and gazed upward.

"Give the man his napkin, Paul," said Rita.

"Yes, or I give you to old ladies," warned Fujiko.

I returned the napkin to the waiter, who took it by one corner with two fingers. He stepped back again, and then carved a large arc along the cobblestone, flaring his nostrils in my direction as he passed, while still managing to wink interestedly at Rita. He disappeared into the crypt, as *Los éxitos de los 70s* (The Best of the '70s) played over the stereo.

WE HAPPENED UPON the Bierzo Wine District after suddenly finding ourselves in a new world of vineyards in, of all places, hilly northern Spain. On a south-facing slope, we saw twisted leafless wine stalks that looked like bulls buried to their necks in flowery meadows.

After about two hours of wending through vineyards, we arrived at the edge of Villafranca, just in time for the communal pilgrim meal at the local *albergue*. We fit ourselves into a multicultural crowd around folding tables set up in the reception area of the hostel. The hostel owner led us in a Spanish prayer, which ended in applause and laughter by those who understood. Fujiko then taught the group the traditional Japanese prayer of thanks: *Itadakimasu*, which means, "I take this."*

"*Itadakimasu*," recited everyone, (or some approximation), and the communal meal began.

There were many familiar faces among the crowd, including the bald businessman with his cellphone from the first night, the Austrian girls, Heraclio of the Infected Toe and boyfriend Fabían, and Helmut and Dolores (with her tube of green muscle paste for him). Other than that, the tables were populated with a mess of other pilgrims, one of whom voiced both the collegial feelings on the surface as well as the undercurrents below.

"Him?" said a tiny Frenchman, patting a giant German on the shoulder. "He is German and I am French. But we are on the Camino, so we are friends."

Trays of fried eggs made their rounds, as did platters of homemade sausage, bread, bowls of communal greens and bottomless carafes of water and wine.

«¿What is *el suyo nombre?*» I asked the bald businessman as he momentarily put his cell phone down. He looked at me and said something unpleasant in Spanish. Heraclio turned red.

"Sometimes you do not want to talk," offered Heraclio's boyfriend, Fabían.

Just then, the cell phone rang. With one hand over his ear, the businessman carried on a conversation at the table. It

---

* Though impossible to translate, *itadakimasu* really means something more complex like: "Thank you Mother Earth, farmers and all who are responsible for preparing this meal for me, including the wiggly organisms I am about to eat."

irritated me to no end, but I couldn't see any point in saying anything. Impolite cellphone use upsets me enough that my own frustrations would highjack any meaningful comment. So I forced myself to smile dumbly instead. Inside though, I ranted about how he might have been connected to the person at the other end, but he had just distanced himself from a nice group of people from all over the world who were gathered under one roof for a fleeting one-time-only engagement.

I was pulled from my pout by Dolores who was clearly upset. "Please to send the bread in the clock's direction," she said. I noticed Rita and Fujiko each passing a basket of bread in opposite directions around the table.

"Please to send the bread in the clock's direction," repeated Dolores.

Rita and Fujiko were both confused and I could see a clash of cultures going on. We don't have rules in Canada about what direction bread goes around the table. Nor do we tend to get upset with a little disorganization. But Dolores's stress, right or wrong, I attributed to a Germanic love of order compounded by genuine pilgrim hunger: she needed bread. Fujiko's stress might have been related to needing to please Dolores without implying that Rita made a mistake. And Rita's might have been caused by someone suggesting she was not keeping order in the first place. What a shame that coming together should be so complicated.

Rita and Fujiko hesitated momentarily and then both passed a basket to the Spanish businessman. He took a piece of bread from Rita but waved at Fujiko dismissively. She smiled a tight smile and sent the bread back toward Dolores's end of the table.

When the businessman's call was through, he reached for Dolores's muscle cream and squeezed it onto a piece of bread like anchovy paste. It took me a moment to register that he was about to eat it. I felt conflicted. The Christian thing to do was to stop him, but it was hard to be Christian when you don't know the Spanish words for "Don't eat the balm." But I did manage to say, *«Atención, es muy picante»* ("Careful, it's very spicy") but not with enough conviction to stop the train wreck from happening.

The Spanish businessman looked at me dismissively, picked up the green sandwich and raised it toward his lips. When I caught myself about to smile, I lowered my gaze to my own plate. But I glanced up in time to see him insert the sandwich into his mouth. Almost immediately he gagged and reached for his paper napkin. Another call came in and he left, looking around as if he was trying to find the culprit. After that, the communal dinner continued without further international incidents.

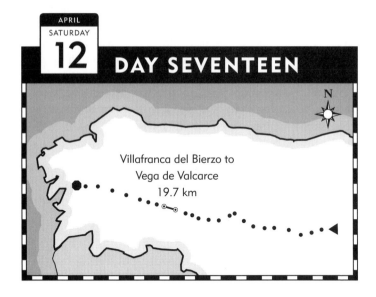

Villafranca del Bierzo to
Vega de Valcarce
19.7 km

N

IN A SMOKY CAFÉ, over repeated servings of yellow cake, I asked Rita what was in store for us for today.

"We have a choice," she explained. "We can give ourselves an ugly but easy walk along a dangerous highway or we can treat ourselves to a gruelling climb over a mountain and enjoy an amazing view." Rita and Fujiko chose the mountain path, figuring the extra effort would be worth it. And so we packed up any leftover yellow cake and wandered through this medieval maze of a town in search of the mountain trailhead. We found it at the opposite end of town, marked by a sign with a message worth noting.

Camino muy duro
Solo para buenos caminantes

"Paul-*san*, what does it mean?" asked Fujiko.

"Loosely translated, it means, "I'd turn back if I were you.""

In the first 15 minutes of our climb along a narrow wooded path, a sheet of clouds completely obscured what had been a uniformly blue sky. But what we lost of the sun's heat, we made up internally, fighting gravity to scale the mountain. I was too winded to talk, but the women somehow found the strength to chat.

"This is brutal," said Rita.

"It is worse in Japan," said Fujiko.

"What could be worse?"

"In Japan there is Buddhist pilgrimage where pilgrim must walk 22 days."

"That's nothing. We're walking for 25," said Rita.

"But Japanese pilgrim must never stop, not even to rest. And if he do, he commit suicide."

"That's crazy," said Rita.

"Why does suffering have to be such a pain?" I asked.

"Life *is* suffering," said Rita, a bit too pleasantly to be convincing.

Fujiko smiled back saying, "Rita-*san*, I have suffering present for you."

Then Fujiko pretended to stomp on one of Rita's blistered feet, barely missing it. Rita jumped out of the way, laughing. Fujiko stomped again, but Rita narrowly escaped. They continued this oddly playful dance for some time. Stomping, jumping and giggling, until Rita skipped away and we followed, laughing some more.

After walking on for some way, I thought to myself how amazing it was that Rita didn't seem to be bothered by her blistered feet. In spite of the pain, she suffered life fully and was better for it. That's the kind of suffering I wouldn't mind having for myself.

Along the narrow ledge of an escarpment, we arrived to find an abandoned, rusting washing machine standing beside the cliff. Who managed to lug it there was anyone's guess. On the machine itself, someone had written a message with indelible ink, which I wrote in my notebook:

Respect the nature you fucking pilgrims.

When we finally arrived at the top, we agreed it had been the most challenging climb yet. Unfortunately there was no reward because the clouds had stolen the view.

Worn down by the steady climb and subsequent descent, the rest of the day's walk seemed to creep along too slowly for me. In every town, I asked if we could stop there for the night, but Rita demanded that we push on. "Tomorrow's climb is worse," she said. "We have to get as far as we can today."

As it turned out, only the smell of fresh bread from a bakery could weaken her resolve. And so in the late afternoon, we stopped in the unusual hamlet of Vega de Valcarce.

Squished between wooded bluffs, the town rests at the foot of a giant bridge that arches across the valley like a concrete rainbow. The bridge carries the A-6, a four-lane highway from Madrid to the Atlantic. Locals must try to ignore its looming presence but the audible hint of traffic passing overhead draws the eye irresistibly upward and away from the otherwise pristine setting below, where stubby horses feed on tall grass in a pasture that borders a stream. Next to that, in the shadow of the bridge, stood the bakery. Once inside, we downed plates of almond cookies covered in powdered sugar.

"Was the suffering worth it?" asked Rita.

"Ah, that was nothing," I replied, the day's ordeal all but forgotten.

We rented rooms in a renovated house across the street but ended up getting the entire place to ourselves. That evening, we started a fire and sat opposite a warm hearth draped with drying laundry. We ate cheese sandwiches, shared a bottle of red wine and a slab of leftover yellow cake.* Around 11 p.m., just as we heard the radiators click off for the night, we scattered to our warm beds before the cold settled in, and slept soundly until morning.

---

* Yellow really was the most distinguishing feature of this cake of all cakes. It was bland but addictive, nondescript but unique. When you walk the Camino, be sure to look for yellow cake.

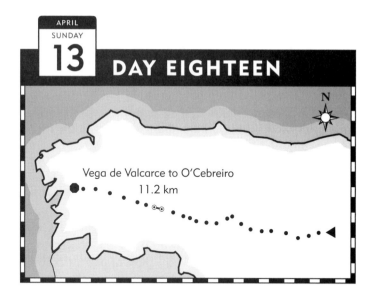

DAY EIGHTEEN

Vega de Valcarce to O'Cebreiro
11.2 km

N

I WOKE UP HAVING DREAMT that I wet the bed, only I hadn't. Thank God. So I relaxed under the warm covers until I began to remember how at the amphibious age of six, wetting the bed had been part of an all but nightly routine that I had not quite outgrown. The year was 1970, and my family had been living in Switzerland, crammed into a two-bedroom apartment. The four boys slept dormitory style in the second bedroom on two single beds and two foldout cots. The four girls slept, two by two, like spoons in a drawer on two daybeds in the den, while my parents watched TV in the master bedroom. My father was a physics professor on sabbatical and had brought us to Europe to live for a year. My mother took a break from teaching piano students back home and instead, taught her eight kids on the apartment's grand piano.

My father decided the boys would rotate beds nightly on a four-day schedule so that nobody would be stuck sleeping on a cot all the time. The rotation went like this: on Day 1, I wet the bed closest to the window. On Day 2, I wet the army cot set up between the two beds. On Day 3, I wet the second single bed. And, on Day 4, I wet the other army cot closest to the bathroom. With four days of drying time between sleeps, the system worked better for me than my brothers. Peter, the second youngest boy, followed my rotation and thus slept nightly in dampness. Poor guy. In just eight days, he developed a skin condition and was prescribed a salve that made his skin turn yellow. My father rethought his initial scheme and I was permanently stationed on the cot closest to the bathroom, while my older brothers rotated among themselves. Until, that is, I learned to master my own bladder and petitioned my father to be re-introduced into the rotation.

Setting such dampish musings aside, I climbed out of bed and went about my morning business. The clanging of water pipes overhead signalled that the women were also awake and preparing for the day. In no time, the three of us were scurrying through the rain to the *panadería*, where Spain's sweetest breakfast would be waiting.

Pigging out on a bakery breakfast was a childhood dream of mine and, on this day, I got to check it off my list. I was just glad my parents were not there to spoil it. Unchecked by their better judgment, I ordered one of everything I wanted, which was almost everything in the display. I pointed at the different exotic cakes, cookies and cream-filled pastries as the clerk's eyes grew to the size of his habit-forming almond cookies.

"Today we climb the mountain," said Rita, tearing out guidebook pages from the previous day's walk and making this day's the new Page 1. "It's supposed to be the toughest climb of the Camino, but it has the most beautiful scenery."

"It might snow!" said Fujiko, looking up from her Japanese guidebook.

I ordered another hot chocolate and a plate of almond cookies. "We're going to need all the sugar we can get to make it to the top," I justified.

"If your teeth fall out you'll have less to carry," said Rita. I smiled from behind a mess of powdered sugar, looking like a second-rate mime.

We gathered our packs and walked out of this sleepy hamlet – one that somehow managed to support two banks, several hotels, places with rooms to rent, a supermarket, a pharmacy and a sign pointing toward an invisible post office.

For 40 minutes, we walked alone, single file or side by side, depending on the road, our changing moods and our own sense of pace. This dance was one we had mastered wordlessly over the previous two and a half weeks, and on this drizzly morning we took to it naturally again. Before leaving Canada, I was afraid that we would be walking together all the time and talking too much. But that had not been the case. In the company of Rita and Fujiko, I had spent long hours plodding along with my own thoughts. It had actually worked out perfectly.

We wound our way through the deep valley, eyeing a low ceiling of clouds that we would soon climb into, although the occasional blue patch offered hope of a view from above. We followed the N-006A and, according to the milepost, were 428 km from somewhere.

Somehow, I wouldn't have missed this day's walk for the world. In Toronto, I hail cabs before walking in the rain. But here, with the right gear, I looked and felt as cozy as an astronaut meandering through a lunar spring. As wet and cold as it was on the outside, I was warm and dry to the core, beneath my many high-tech layers.

Across a narrow stream, a man fished for trout. Behind him, a narrow poplar forest hugged a steep mountainside. From within the woods, a symphony of clanging cowbells could be heard, announcing that a field's worth of cows were grazing invisibly in the shadows.

"Another glorious day of walking in the rain," I said, except this time I was not being sarcastic.

"In seven, maybe eight days, we'll be in Santiago," said Rita.

"We walk very, very fast," added Fujiko.

"One more week and we'll be looking for excuses to get off the couch: Places to go, people to see," I added.

Walking on in silence, it was as if I had three perspectives at that moment: I was anxious to make it to Santiago; I did not want the walking to end; and I was ready to go home.

ABOUT THREE QUARTERS of an hour later, trudging past me along the steepest, narrowest, muddiest, most dismal stretch of trail, Rita declared amicably, "Well you got the suffering you wanted." Rather than reply, I thought to myself instead: No, I love this. I'm not suffering at all.

Determined not to sweat, I inched along. Step by step, I pondered the mountainside opposite as it intermittently showed itself through drifting gaps in the fog. I let Rita and Fujiko move on ahead, wanting some space for myself. As I watched them disappear around a bend, I was struck by a tremendous pain in my chest.

Is this the suffering I hoped for?

Even though I'm a self-diagnosed hypochondriac, I still leaned against the mountain and ran through a mental checklist of what it might have been but wasn't:

Reflux esophagitis?

Gastritis?

Pleuritis?

Costochondritis?

Detritus?

Or maybe this was the big one – a heart attack!

On the facing hillside, from behind heavy shifting clouds, I caught glimpses of pastures afire in golden greens. Refined-looking cows lazed about as if on recess at a bovine finishing school. The landscape was so arresting it was a crime not to stare. Frozen in awe, I couldn't move forward.

This was far too beautiful a countryside to leave behind, I thought to myself.

"Draw this. Sketch this. Share it with others," said a voice inside my head.

"And then what? Stick it on a friend's fridge with magnets, like I'm some pre-schooler?" I asked out loud. The pain of wanting to draw nearly knocked me over.

Minutes passed. The pain didn't.

Then the voice inside my head said, "Patience, my love, for tomorrow we die."

What?

Cows in the pasture facing me lacked the sensitivity to look away and allow me my privacy.

"Patience, my love, for tomorrow we die."

My armpits started to sweat. I caught the whiff of an over-ripe pear emanating from the gaps in my raincoat around my face. An odd mix of thoughts and feelings came over me. They emanated from the pain in the chest, and were connected in inexpressible ways to my whole life and sense of being.

THE VOICE: The joy of beauty. The *suffering* of joy. Live the joy of life for no other reason than it has been given to you … and then … one day …

THE RELUCTANT PILGRIM: Yes? Come on. Out with it.

THE VOICE: … It leaves you …

THE RELUCTANT PILGRIM: Wha – ?

THE VOICE: Hopefully before you have turned your back in bitterness or despair.

More intense pain.

THE VOICE: Your heart wants only love. Your heart needs only love. Your heart knows only love.

I looked again at the other hillside and held my breath.

THE VOICE: Patience, my love, for tomorrow we die. This is not sadness for what has happened but sadness for what has *wanted* to happen. You are mourning life that has wanted to be lived.

Silence. Birdsong.

THE VOICE: Patience, my love, for tomorrow we die.

THE RELUCTANT PILGRIM: ENOUGH ALREADY!

I shouted this at the top of my lungs, my voice echoing in all directions for the whole valley to hear.

THE RELUCTANT PILGRIM: I WANT TO LIVE MY LIFE ALREADY!

ECHO: I WANT TO LIVE MY LIFE ALREADY!

Already! *Already!* Already. Already.

Across the valley, two cows had been watching without once shifting their gaze. But suddenly they shook their heads and the bells around their necks clanged. I took this as a mystical sign, while ignoring eight other cows in the herd that had been mooning me the entire time.

Then I started to cry. Uncontrollably. I was happy; unspeakably happy to be feeling connected to the mountains across the way that drifted in and out of view through the fog, to the clouds that hung heavy at times and then glowed green as they thinned out, to the storm that was threatening, to the cold air against my face and to the pungent smell of pine that carved its own path.

I was fiercely alive. My chest ached from it. And at the same time, I was filled with the knowledge that some undetermined day, against my will, I will have to say goodbye. The connection will be lost, and I'll be adrift. But at this time, at least, the moment was filled with a boundless joy that felt intensely "me" and "more than me" at the same time. Every cell breathed. Every thought burned. As much as this walk had been tedious, uncomfortable and frustrating, I desperately needed to find ways to enjoy it, because this was all there was.

As the clouds swallowed the cows whole and rain suddenly fell in torrents, I turned to continue climbing. The deluge turned the Camino into a trail of goo and sludge. If my feet hadn't sunk up to my ankles with every step, I would have slipped and fallen into globs of cow dung along the stone-lined path.

My heart hurt in a good way.

Jacqueline, a French woman *d'un certain âge* appeared, walking the Camino in the wrong direction.

"Where are you going?" I asked.

"Back to my own country," she replied, glowing. I watched her retreat confidently down the mountain path as though stepping into existence a new spoke of the Camino.

There was a spring in my step, despite having to continue through the mud. When I arrived at a stone building where I found Rita and Fujiko's ponchos draped over their backpacks on the front porch, I rubbed my feet on the *bienvenido* mat and entered. Inside, I found them seated in front of a fire, warming the place with their familiar smiles.

"I want to live my life already?" asked Rita. "What was that all about?" I smiled the tiniest hint of a smile for several moments, not knowing what to say.

"Never mind; I get it," she said, and returned to her cheese sandwich and hot tea. I ordered the same and joined Rita and Fujiko in front of the fire.

A TV was suspended in the corner over the door where *The Simpsons* was playing in Spanish. Rita and I laughed because it was not in English. Fujiko laughed because it was not in Japanese. A Swiss woman laughed because it was not in German, while the Spanish waitress shook her head, wondering what was so funny. We stayed to the end of *Los Simpsons* but headed out immediately afterward because Rita said there were limited accommodations on top of the mountain.

THOUGH IT WAS RAINING when we sat down, when we left it was snowing big thick Christmassy flakes. The wind had picked up and the temperature had fallen 10 degrees. Snowflakes blew about festively like bite-sized portions of cotton candy.

We each wore everything we had. For me that meant the sleeping bag was up my sleeves and bunched into a beer-belly-like ball in the middle of my raincoat.

"Homeru Simpusonu!" said Fujiko, laughing and pointing at me.* Dolores and Helmut, arriving to warm themselves in the bar, did a double-take, which made me think I probably did look like Homer.

Fifteen minutes later, a stone marker said we were leaving the province of León and entering Galicia, where St. James is sentenced to an eternity of uninvited houseguests.

"What is Galicia like?" I asked Rita.

"From what I gather, it snows a lot," said Rita, looking around.

"And very, very foggy," added Fujiko.

"Very, very funny. But what does the guidebook say?"

----

* "Homer Simpson" in Japanese is *Homeru Simpusonu*. Honest, it is; just as "Mac-Donald's" is *Macudonarudo*.

"Oh, I don't read ahead," joked Rita. "That would be cheating."

"Live today, tomorrow maybe die," said Fujiko, with mock seriousness.

Three hundred metres further on, a stone marker read: Santiago 152 km. Shortly after that, we arrived without warning at the summit, which had been concealed by the fog.

"Who would have guessed the end would be so near?" I asked no one in particular.

AFTER CHECKING INTO A ROCKY HOTEL at the summit, I headed to my room and ran a steaming bath. Moments after lowering myself into it, like a piece of thawing meat, I imagined that Bill Maher, the comedian and creator of the documentary *Religulous*, was interviewing me.

> Bill M: Help me out here because you seem like a reasonable man. But you don't go to church, and if I might be so bold, I don't think you even believe in God. So what on Earth possessed you to go on this Catholic pilgrimage in the first place?
>
> Paul H: Friends asked me, and once I said yes, I couldn't say no.
>
> Bill M: No, no, no, no, no. That's a lot o' malarkey. Sorry.
>
> Paul H: I felt obligated!
>
> Bill M: People bring chicken soup to sick friends because they feel obligated but they don't walk for a month to do it. People give money to lousy street performers because they feel obligated, but they don't fly to Madrid to do it. People eat what's on their plate when they're over for dinner, but they don't ask for seconds if they don't like it. Okay, religious obligation aside, did you meet any other pilgrim walking 25 days out of obligation?
>
> Paul H: No.
>
> Bill M: So what makes you so special that you say yes when no would have made so much more sense?
>
> Paul H: I wanted to move my hips for 25 days.

Bill M: That is the gayest thing I've ever heard. My friend, that is called a very long orgasm. And if you find a church that sanctions one of those, call me because at least that church has it going on. So why did you really go?

Paul H: I wanted to do something fearless.

Bill M: Fearless?

Paul H: Walking the Camino when I usually run from religion.

Bill M: Stupid might be a better descriptor.

Paul H: How about stupidly fearless?

Bill M: Okay, I'll give you that.

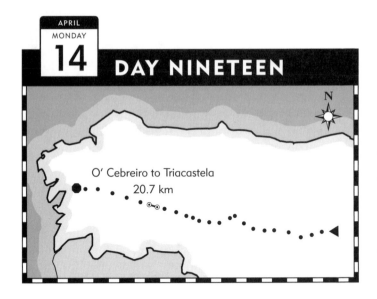

O' Cebreiro to Triacastela
20.7 km

N

"RITA," I ASKED. "Has anything extraordinary happened to you on the Camino?"

"Of course," she replied. "But I'm not about to tell you about it. You would think I was crazy."

After a few moments, she asked: "Did something happen to you yesterday?"

Several more seconds passed, and then I pursed my lips slightly and nodded my head four times.

"There is no point in telling me," Rita said smiling. "I already think you're crazy."

And then she added, "Are you okay?"

She took my silent smile as a yes and then patted me twice on the chest with her open hand. "Good."

Soon afterwards, we were outside and began to proceed through a modern version of the Flintstones' town of Bedrock, with its uniform stone walls, slate roofs and green shutters. As we arrived at the scenic viewing point, I was reminded of the spectacular sunrise that Rita, Fujiko and I had shared atop

Mount Fuji. This morning's sun rested on the horizon like a ceremonial gong, just as it had then. It glowed through a dancing pink fog that burned like embers at its edges, while overhead the air was fresh, cerulean and cold. Shoulder to shoulder we looked back and witnessed the unveiling of yesterday's journey through the thinned-out haze behind us. Eventually we saw the A-6 and spotted the bridge we knew arched over the bakery. It seemed submerged at the bottom of a deep dry sea. "It's amazing how high we've climbed," said Rita.

I sat on a bench and looked out at this picture. Rita sat next to me, removed a boot and attended to blisters that all but covered the back of her right foot.

"Must be painful," I said.

"You get used to it," she said. "There's nothing I can do about it."

Fujiko circled us gingerly as she broke the surface of the frozen puddles with the toe of her boot. Then she crunched across frozen grass as birds chirped overhead and mimicked the beep-beep-beep sound of the garbage trucks that had backed up in León. I removed the black marker and my notepad from my backpack and began to draw, as the colours, shapes and smells of the land we had walked through flooded over me. It was cold, but my fingers felt alive. My heart seemed to hurt.

It was a gentle echo of yesterday's episode that resurfaced with a stubborn urge to create. With a few scribbled lines, I attempted to bring back the church where Fujiko sang the Japanese sutra on our second day of walking. I doodled the path of the Camino as a little voice inside my head whis-pered, "Let there be hills!" I complied and, with equal speed, I drew a stand of poplars and recalled how they had floated pensively on their tiny trunks, like caterpillars meditating on their own shadows. For a few moments, I lost myself and stared at the naïve little drawing. It was a world that I created from another world that I may have known only briefly but had found a place in my memory.

As Rita finished re-mummifying her feet, she looked over at me, and I put my marker and notebook away. Something had woken in me, and I had no intention of letting it go.

On the far side of town, we climbed along a road that was to lead to the crucifix at the mountain's peak. Then we descended along a forest path that threaded through patches of tiny sun-starved daffodils. After about 2 km, the forest gave way to a meadow where we arrived at a T-junction, sans arrows, sans markers, sans shells, sans anything.

"What now?"

"I don't know," said Rita. "This is not in the guidebook."

Groups of pilgrims emptied out of the forest in ones, twos, threes and fours, each stopping at the junction, consulting guidebooks and looking about. The Germans' books said to turn right; the guidebooks belonging to the French said to turn left; and ours said nothing at all. When two Swiss women that we had seen repeatedly walking in the wrong direction turned left, we turned right and followed the Germans.

Struck by how the landscape seemed to have relaxed in front of us, we descended without looking back at the snow-capped mountains that we had trailed and scaled for weeks. Without us realizing it, they disappeared from view forever as we embraced a new world before us, where the ground stretched downward toward a patchwork of gently rolling wooded hills, verdant pastures and speckled towns.

As we descended, we listened to the phantom whir of automobiles snaking along the side of the mountain far beneath us. The day had worn on without me having given much attention to the landscape around me. It was as though the movement of walking had become more important than the scenery. Rita continually restated her estimated time of arrival until around 3 p.m., when we trailed through an incandescent field of mustard, stepped along a lane of medieval farmsteads and entered the town of Triacastela. German shepherds lazed along the walls soaking up the sun. As we passed, they raised an inquisitive brow before closing their eyes with a harrumph and snuggling their chins into the warm gravel road.

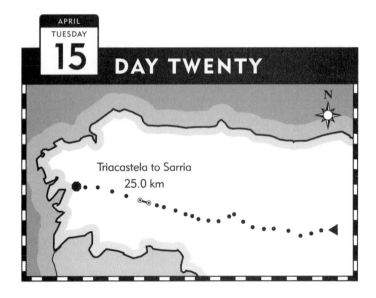

Triacastela to Sarria
25.0 km

"TODAY, I'LL DISCOVER the meaning of life," I thought to myself, and as Castilian roosters cried out their familiar *Ki-kiri-ki*, I actually believed I would.

Out on the trail, less meditative pilgrims passed me as I plodded along pensively: the two directionally challenged Swiss women walked by as one lectured the other on the virtues of certainty. They smiled at me perfunctorily and then nattered on up the hill.

The snoring Irishman, whom we had not seen for days (or heard from for nights), wished me a *Buen Camino*. And then he asked, "Where are you from, by the way?"

"Canada," I replied.

"Oh," he said. "I like to think of Canadians as American-lite."

"I guess that makes you British-lite, eh?" He kept going, without looking back.

Next, Dolores strode by, trailed by Helmut who laboured up the hill in fits and starts. Hands on knees, he stopped and gasped for air for a few moments, and then dragged himself with his ski poles a little further before he stopped to catch his breath again. Helmut looked worn. Still, he climbed to the ridge nonetheless and rested with his wife, who was waiting where the forest ended. There the wooded trail opened up to hills that rolled gently in every direction.

The countryside looked as though someone had taken a Cézanne painting, pulled at the edges of the landscape playfully and warped the perspective into a wonky masterpiece. Faraway towns dotted the countryside, as did cows on distant hills: in the valley below, a thin patch of fog was so smooth that it resembled an ice rink on a still morning.

"The meaning of life. Now what could that be?" I wondered. In the absence of a quick reply, I sat on a log next to a shaded brook, pulled out my notebook and marker, and drew.

Paul's Illustrated Camino

Me   Rita   Fujiko

It's a solitary journey.

But each one plays his or her part.

Birds chirp.

Fyu fyu fi fi chi chi chi chika chika chika

Friends eat picnics.

Fujiko sings in a church.

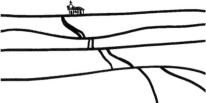

And they walk

for days

across the Meseta.

It's always the same Camino, but it looks different.

The Camino.

The Camino.

The Camino.

The Camino.

The highest point of the
Camino.

Washing Machine on
mountain trail.
(I added the clothesline ... it
wasn't there.)

And after walking in the rain enough, they become like a team.

They follow special markers across northern Spain,

collecting experiences along the way.

A PANG OF HUNGER reminded me that I needed to eat lunch. We had bought supplies but never made any plans to meet. Suddenly, the meaning of life could wait, as herding Rita and Fujiko like a sheepdog became priority *número uno*. I picked up the pace until I was speeding past the pilgrims that had passed me earlier: Dolores and Helmut, the Irishman, and the two Swiss women who were (at least momentarily) headed in the right direction.

Eventually, I caught up to Fujiko, who sat side-saddle on a rock next to a pond. She looked like a mermaid enjoying the view. "I rest a while," she exclaimed almost triumphantly.

Fujiko agreed that lunch would be a good idea and we trekked on briskly, soon passing the five Germans we had not seen in five days.

The trail carved its way through woods and alongside pastures. It was an ancient road, lined with tall stone walls. Water from the previous day's rain ran over shiny stones and turned the walkway, in places, into a rushing stream, which we waded through. Forty-five minutes later, Rita appeared in the distance, across a valley and walking at an athletic clip. Plugged into her MP3 player, she was in another world. As we climbed the ridge and slowly gained on her, Fujiko and I, like nomadic escape artists, slipped out of our outer layers of clothing without removing our backpacks or slowing down. The day was not altogether warm, but the brisk walk made it feel that way.

We finally caught up to Rita, whom we found sitting in the sun outside a country chapel. A sheepdog – all tongue – sat beside her. Side by side, they stared out at the countryside like old friends who didn't need to speak to enjoy each other's company. Cows from the farm behind broke out onto the street to the cries of rubber-booted women who flashed sticks in the air. The sheepdog retracted its tongue, glanced up at Rita and then swung into action. It barked and nipped at the heals of the livestock, bolted this way and that, and prevented any independently-minded cows from escaping to the open road of the Camino. With the cows safely in their pasture, the dog returned to Rita's side and watched in silent disbelief as we feasted contentedly on cheese and orange sandwiches made with dry bread. The sheepdog looked at us and tilted its head. Then it ran up the lane to its home, where lunch was likely to be more appetizing.

"What is the meaning of life?" I asked Rita and Fujiko.

Rita's cheese and orange sandwich hovered in mid-air as she thought. "Experiences," she said.

"Is that all?" I asked.

"I don't know," said Rita. "Do I look like the Dalai Lama?"

"Life means many things," offered Fujiko. "Today may be different than tomorrow. I think Paul-*san* must answer question himself."

"But I don't have an answer," I countered.

Fujiko shrugged her shoulders as if she knew something but wasn't willing or able to say.

Just as I was about to fire another question, the flock of Germans arrived. "*Guten Apetit!*" they said more or less in unison.

"Thank you," we said back, smiling.

The handsomest one, whose blue eyes saw only Rita, smiled affectionately at her. Unable to speak English, he cleared his throat before puffing on his cigarette and feigned an aloof disinterest in life. He looked out at the pleasant countryside as though bored by it and then turned back toward Rita to offer her a cigarette.

"No thank you," she said, a little too abruptly. "I don't smoke." He looked confused and slightly hurt.

One of his friends grabbed him by the shoulder and pulled him back into the fold. For several minutes, the Germans carried on laughing among themselves before they wished us a *Buen Camino* and headed down the road in a haze of smoke.

"Life is about wonderful experiences," said Rita. "Too bad we can't live them all."

After lunch, we spread out and walked alone through a countryside that flattened out even more than earlier. I found it oddly reassuring that after I spent the afternoon asking myself about the meaning of life no answer came. Without a set meaning, life could be lived more deeply, it seemed to me. I was free to live life as it is – one great big question mark. And in that, I could open myself to experience the profound curiosity and awe that are what this incredible adventure begs of me. Without rigid beliefs, my journey was free to take any infinite number of unexpected turns. It felt more like living a life than playing a role that someone else had written for me.

BY MID-AFTERNOON, we arrived on the edge of Sarria and checked into the first place we saw, *Pension de Pedra*. After the cult of laundry and pursuant rituals of showers and naps, we congregated in the bar for drinks before supper. Seated at tables made from giant slices of tree trunks, we ordered drinks from Lucio, who delivered them with repeated winks.

"Is it a twitch or is he flirting with us?" I asked.

"I'm not sure," said Rita. "Either way, he's charming."

"What is that?" I asked suddenly, struck by a peculiar and shiny knick-knack on the bar.

«Botafumeiro», said Lucio winking again.

«¿Botafumeiro?» repeated Rita as she looked about. "But it's so small!"

"But what is it?" I repeated.

Rita read from her guidebook, "The *Botafumeiro* is a famous thurible and one of the world's largest censers weighing approximately 80 kg."

"What is she saying?" I asked Lucio blankly.

"It is for incense for smelly pilgrims," explained Lucio.

"I read about it before I left home," said Rita, before explaining further. "In the Cathedral of Santiago there's a giant incense burner just like this. For over 400 years, they have lit it during special pilgrim Masses. Normally incense is for prayer, but in Santiago, they swing this thing up to the rafters so the smoke hides the stench of grimy pilgrims."

"A giant air freshener!" I exclaimed.

«Sí», said Lucio, as he smiled and winked again.

"Only today they don't light it at every Mass," continued Rita. "Only for bus groups; apparently it costs a lot of money."

Lucio nodded his head and rubbed his thumb against his fingers – the international sign for *mucho dinero*.

"So let me get this right," I said, "If you pay a lot of money to the Roman Catholic Church, they will gladly insult your sense of personal hygiene by swinging a giant air freshener over your head?"

"Basically," said Rita.

"How much?" I asked Lucio.

«*¿Qué?*» he replied.

"I want to do it." The thought that I had the power to pay Rome to swing a giant-sized version of this thing over the smelly pilgrims in the Cathedral of Santiago struck me as an irresistibly cool idea.

"Do what, Paul-*san*?" asked Fujiko.

"I want to pay to swing the giant deodorant," I said.

«*Botafumeiro*», corrected Lucio.

"It's really expensive," warned Rita.

"Follow me," said Lucio, winking and then heading out the front door. He led me to the municipal tourism office, conveniently located next door. Inside, Lucio explained my intentions to the attractive but artificial blonde at the desk. She looked at me and smiled, and then spun in her chair to type away furiously at her computer. Within moments, she dialled a number, explained something in Spanish and then handed me the phone.

"You wish to order the sacrament of the *Botafumeiro*?" asked the voice on the other end.

"Yes," I said.

"What day do you arrive in Santiago?" she asked.

"Sunday," I replied.

"That is difficult," she said, "The *Botafumeiro* requires 12 *tiraboleiros*. It is Tuesday, sir, and I only have five days to gather 12 priests."

"Still..." I replied, imagining how priests must be crawling out of the woodwork in Santiago.

"What is the name of your group?" she asked.

"The name of my group?" I stalled.

"Yes, the name of your group."

I paused. "The reluctant pilgrims."

"Where are you from?"

"Canada."

"Ah, America," she sighed. "It will cost 240 euros."

Silence. "*Señor* Canada, are you there?"

"Yes ... sorry," I replied. I was silent because of a complex mix of thoughts and emotions. To be sure, €240 was a lot of money. But I was also feeling guilty for behaving so mischievously with the Church.

"You will wire the money to the Archdiocese of Santiago by three o'clock on Thursday," she said. I gave the woman on the phone my email address so that the Archdiocese of Santiago could send me the necessary paperwork. I said goodbye and hung up.

I left the tourism office with a lingering sense of guilt, which I quickly justified. I might have been playing a joke on the Catholic Church by ordering the *Botafumeiro* for non-religious reasons, but at least it was at my expense.

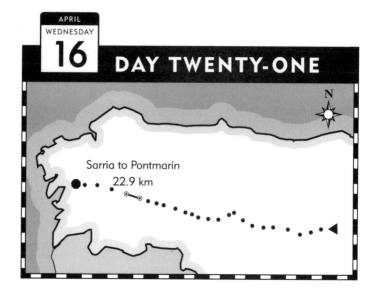

WITH MILITARY PRECISION, we gathered our knapsacks and stepped silently onto the street. Like infantry that had orders to take the neighbouring hills by oh-eight-hundred hours, we marched toward the elevated central square of Sarria, just over 100 km to Santiago. In spite of the early hour, most of the shops were open and merchants waited confidently for pilgrims who – having taken over this town – needed to stop in for flashlights, walking sticks, guidebooks, gloves, socks, or waterproof anything. Coffee shop windows were awash with the colourful gear of pilgrims who sat inside on tall stools, fuelling their animated selves with strong Spanish coffee.

Able-bodied pilgrims are required to walk, at minimum, the last 100 km to Santiago in order to receive a pilgrim's certificate and to be anointed officially as one of the transient faithful. For this reason, Sarria was the starting point for many, whose bravado I attributed partly to the freshness of the day, partly to the fact that they didn't know the repetitive weariness of the pilgrim routine and partly because they would likely arrive after walking only a few days. We passed several lines of pilgrims who colourfully littered the street as they waited their turn to enter for coffee and mutual congratulations.

After we left town, Rita, Fujiko and I gradually spread out until we each were walking alone and out of sight of the others.

About an hour into the morning's walk, an apparition stopped me cold: in the middle of nowhere, next to an untilled field, a Coke machine was plugged into a lamppost. The machine was so out of place, so otherworldly, that I was struck as dumb as Bernadette in Lourdes, France, when the Virgin Mary appeared to her out of the blue, on February 11, 1858, scaring the bejesus out of her.

A frightful sight? A miracle? A mirage?

The Coke machine greedily accepted the one-euro coins I inserted, so it must have been real. In exchange, it released a bottle of DASANI brand water. I twisted off the plastic cap and drank the cool 333 ml in one uninterrupted go. It was so good that I repeated the process and drank a second bottle, which according to the label, was filtered five times before leaving the factory. *Purely refreshing.*

I continued along the Camino and began slowly accelerating at the quiet urging of my bladder, until I reached a point where two retaining walls sealed off the trail between untilled fields. About 150 metres along this inescapable throughway, I was unable to hold it in any longer and was forced to accept the call of nature. Hemmed in by the retaining walls, I had no recourse but to guiltily empty myself of approximately two bottles worth of water onto the Camino.

"Uh-oh," I said, as I spied the official "Santiago 100 km" stone marker a metre away. I felt terrible, but I was unable to close the floodgates. At the foot of the milestone was another makeshift shrine, featuring flowers, poetry-etched stones and crucifixes braided devoutly out of dead twigs, all of which were being baptized by a stream of approximately 666 ml of liquid rolling down a gentle slope originating from where I stood. Behind me, the pack of Germans, including the one with eyes for Rita, entered the narrows under a permanent cloud of cigarette smoke.

"Next rest area is 10 km," I said, trying to make light of the fact that I had just unwittingly defaced this key milestone. After quickly assessing the situation, the Germans looked at me as if I was insane. I tried to smile back like I wasn't. "Just watering the flowers!" I offered.

They disappeared under puffs of disapproving smoke. Not sure what to do, I counted to a hundred and then followed sheepishly behind.

AROUND NOON, I found Rita and Fujiko seated at a plastic table on a sunny patio, just as the posse of Germans was leaving.

"Someone peed on the 100-km marker," said Rita.

"That's terrible," I said.

"*Furyou!*" said Fujiko.

"What about me?" I asked.

"Not you; *furyou*," repeated Fujiko, and explained that it's the Japanese word for mischief-maker. It was unclear whether they knew it had been me, and I decided to leave it that way.

"What's the special?" I asked, quickly changing the subject.

"Chicken," said Fujiko. Two roosters crowed cockily from the tabletop next to us.

"I'm having those two," said Rita. "Just to get them to shut up."

As we were within 100 km of Santiago, pilgrim rush hour lasted all day, and every table inside and out was taken. Waiting to be served, we met 82-year-old Gertrude from the Netherlands who had returned to leave her husband's ashes behind. We met two men in fatigues who were on a mission to walk 50 km a day. And a blind man arrived, his hand on the shoulder of an obese man who walked with his own oxygen tank. It was an odd bunch. But I was a part of it, too.

AS WE APPROACHED PONTMARÍN, the day was both winding down and cooling down. We rounded a bend to face a flock of sheep being led home just like us. "Follow me," said Rita, scattering the herd as she ran up the middle. The sheep bleated *b-a-a-a-h* piteously as they tried to clear the stone walls of the Camino, many too fat to do so. The shepherd didn't seem to mind and wished us the Camino's standard greeting.

Minutes later, as the sheep sounds trickled away behind us, we arrived at one end of a high bridge. It stretched across an artificial lake, the result of a dam built in 1962. On the other side was a town of about 2,000, Pontmarín, which had been disassembled and then put back together on higher ground when the lake was formed.

Even though this information was written in every guidebook, it was what most pilgrims talked about that day at lunch, hungry for something new to say to each other besides "Where are you from?" and "How far are you walking today?" Being able to spout local history, particularly about something just around the corner, can elevate an average pilgrim to elite status. Find a way of retelling local lore and you could become a bit of a Camino celebrity.

As we arrived in the main square, Fujiko pointed up excitedly to a boxy Romanesque church. Before she had a chance to speak I repeated what I had overheard at lunch. "The Romanesque church of San Nicolás was taken apart and reassembled, piece by piece, above flood lines. San Nicolás is now the world's largest reassembled 3D puzzle of a box."

Just then, the doors of the church groaned open and the blackness of its interior was revealed. A coffin appeared to float in the doorway until pallbearers stepped forward and we could see that a funeral had ended. The procession inched solemnly across the cobblestone square, with gladioli slipping off the wooden casket from time to time. Children kicked at the fallen blooms before getting their heads slapped by women dressed in black. Men placed hats on hearts while puffing surreptitiously on cigarettes. The procession exited the square, then headed down the main columned street which we had just travelled.

Those of us left behind stood respectfully silent for several moments and then sprang back to life as though nothing had happened. But it was hard to dismiss it entirely. I couldn't help but wonder what it would be like when my time comes and I'm carried off. When my 104-year-old grandmother passed away, she was surrounded by four generations who had gathered to say goodbye to her, the fifth. Since I have no children of my own, I was afraid my own funeral would not be quite so well peopled. Still, I hoped that I might get a scaled-down version of a family funeral, where somebody's kids would kick gladioli in my honour.

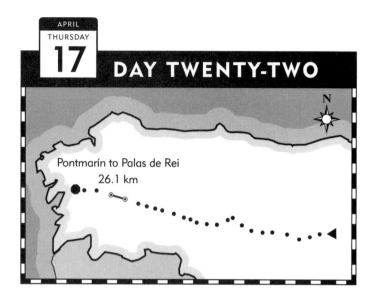

APRIL
THURSDAY
17 DAY TWENTY-TWO

Pontmarín to Palas de Rei
26.1 km

N

AS WE HEADED INTO another stormy day, we crossed paths with a brood of orthodox pilgrims – the kind that only stayed in hostels (they don't seem to believe in hotels). I was a little jealous of their apparent closeness to God but did notice how distant they appeared to be with each other. I smiled and wished them a *Buen Camino*, which rang false. As the rainy day could attest: it was going to be anything but.

"There's nothing to do but walk," said Rita, as she tore out the previous day's pages from her guidebook and tossed them into a bin. Every day since Burgos, Rita had removed the previous day's pages. It made her guidebook increasingly lighter to carry, and now the book had only a few pages left.

"Today is one of the longest days we'll walk," said Rita. "I suggest we break it up. After breakfast, we think of it as a completely new day. After lunch, we think of it as another day still. If we can find other places to rest, we will. That will break the day up even more."

Rita's plan worked perfectly. We walked intermittently in the rain and then rested in a café, a bar and a restaurant along the way. In between, we followed a major two-lane highway that cut through farmed forests that were so perfectly planted as to be utterly unremarkable.

After 22 days of walking, I had to admit how compelling tedium had become. Boredom, I realized, was like a drug. It was an anesthetic that made rising, eating, walking, washing, and lying awake at night oddly fantastical. I walked through inanimate landscapes that were transformed almost imperceptibly, step by step, quite often from one mediocre vista to another.

In the late afternoon, we rested in a bar with a crowd of Australians who were bussing it to Santiago without walking so much as a kilometre. Part of me wanted to hop onboard with them but I had grown determined to follow through with my Camino promises completely.

We also took a small break, visiting a small country chapel the size of a one-car garage. We entered rather hesitantly, as it was dark and smelled of urine. As our eyes adjusted to the damp gloom, we could see that its tiny square windows had been knocked out and its interior walls were all but completely desecrated by graffiti. It had a mud floor and a sleeping bag lay in one corner. I faced the stone altar for several moments feeling that I should offer a prayer of apology for what others had done.

As I stepped back outside, I was reminded how the churches along the Camino seemed often violated or ignored. Other than the cathedrals, their doors had been frequently locked tight, as though God wasn't home, giving us no choice but to pass them by. But those times when we did find the doors open, there were sadly too many signs of neglect – or worse – destruction. It was an oddity of the Camino that pilgrims travel so far to do good and yet largely ignore, and occasionally deface, the cornerstones of their experience – the churches themselves.

Rita seemed unwilling to move on. Through the open door of the shrine, I watched her contemplate a plastic statuette of the Virgin Mary resting on the altar. Potato-chip bags and other litter surrounded it. Rita slowly raised her hand to the Virgin Mary's. She stood palm to miniature palm for several moments. Then she turned and walked out, gently closing the chapel door behind her.

"This is the place," said Rita. She removed her pack and knelt on the ground to unlace her boots, pulling them off at the heels, one at a time, and grimacing slightly as she did. She tied her boots together, returned to the chapel, and hung them over the iron door handles. "I hate to leave them behind, but they're no good to me anymore," she sighed. "Somebody's feet will find them comfortable."

As she put on her running shoes, which at this point would be entrusted to walk her the rest of the way to Santiago, Rita looked back at her boots one last time. Rita's modest contribution to the church and to the benefit of some fellow foot-sore pilgrim hung in silent contrast to the disrespect the chapel had previously suffered.

DURING THE "FIFTH" DAY of walking (having stopped four times already today according to Rita's scheme), my mind drifted back to Catherine, the Irish woman. I had met her on the second morning – the real second morning of the Camino. We spoke over breakfast, way back in Hornillos del Camino, and Catherine hadn't liked my asking why she was walking, feeling it was too personal a question. Twenty days later, I could not get her out of my mind.

It was as though she was walking with me and we were having the conversation I wish we could have had but didn't.

"Why are you walking the Camino?" I asked again.

"Every couple of years I retreat to the Camino to return to myself," replied the imaginary Catherine. "The walking challenges me, the scenery stills me, the weather infuriates me, the silence soothes me. Put it all together and it makes me feel whole."

"What have *you* learned so far?" asked the illusory Catherine, returning my volley.

"What have I learned? I've learned that not believing in facts doesn't make them any less real," I began. "And choosing to believe doesn't make something real either. But I do believe in make-believe: I believe in making something imaginary come to life through art. In that way, I am a part of creation.

And I can create my life, my relationships, my future, insofar as I'm able to interact with others – and provided the world around me cooperates."

"What else?" pursued Catherine so clearly that I wondered if I was conjuring her up or whether this was a spooky instance of extra-sensory perception.

"Sometimes chocolate really does taste good with anchovies," I added.

"Seriously."

"You have to take what you've got and make it work."

"What about your friends?"

"Rita and Fujiko?"

"*Yes.*"

"We don't talk much, yet we work well together."

"We're all in this together," offered Catherine. "And yet the journey itself is walked alone."

"I agree," I added. "Oh, and uh – I believe the world would be a better place if we all wore built-in underwear."

"You're not being serious again," admonished Catherine.

"I am, sort of. It's about making do with less, which is easy to do, provided you have enough."

"So then what's next?"

"I'm not finished yet. I guess I plan to implicate myself into my own life and take responsibility more for where I end up."

"Bravo," said Catherine. "Do you finally know *why* you're walking?"

"No, I don't. But I'm more comfortable with not knowing, and I'm curious to find out."

As the Camino snaked its way through the damp shadows of giant trees and rain delivered a heavy scent of pine, our connection was broken.

About 30 minutes later, Rita, Fujiko and I arrived in Palas de Rei at around 4 p.m. We marched into town along with an army of newbie pilgrims that crowded its sidewalks, loitered on its street corners and infiltrated its grocery stores.

I left the women to run their errands and headed to the bank to wire money to the Archdiocese of Santiago to pay for the *Botafumeiro*. But when I got there, the door wouldn't open. "Damn!"

A little pipsqueak of a Spanish woman pushed past me, reached up and rang a doorbell. There was a buzzing sound and the door clicked open. She passed through, looking over her shoulder so I wouldn't follow.

Once the door locked, I pressed the button myself. The door clicked and I entered.

A doorbell in a bank? I half-expected to find mattresses inside, under which the locals hid their money. I wasn't far off. Photos of pastoral settings hung from plain beige walls. Three men at keyboards, lit by overhead lamps, sat at simple desks arranged haphazardly. Surrounded by piles of loose papers, they busily entered data. The place seemed more like a horse betting operation than a bank.

«Send-o euros *al* Santiago electronic-*amente por favor*», I said as I placed a slip of paper that itemized the archdiocese's account numbers before one of the clerks.

«*Si Señor*», he said reading the note and smiling.

I handed the clerk €240 in fresh unmarked bills. Moments later, I returned to the street, my spirits and wallet lighter.

TO ESCAPE THE CROWD, we chose a deserted tavern hidden in the basement of a nearby hotel, where a young waitress absolutely charmed us by rolling her eyes whenever we tried to speak Spanish. For dessert, I ordered the traditional Santiago tart – a famous almond cake indigenous to Galicia so buttery sweet that it was worth walking 22 days to find it.

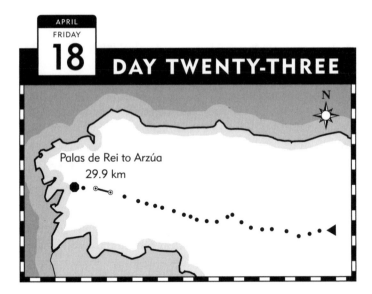

N

Palas de Rei to Arzúa
29.9 km

WE WERE SITTING IN A BAR, having sought sanctuary from the worst day of rain so far. The bar was called *Zwei Deutsche*, which means "Two Germans", although there were about 20 of them squished into that place. They may have been German anarchists, since they'd refused to put their wet things in the back hallway as instructed. As a result, a small lake was pooling at our feet.

A special news bulletin was playing on the TV. More than 5 cm of rain had fallen and the newscasters were warning that there was more to come. The worst rainfall in years had turned Spain into one giant puddle, and the arid people of Madrid were in a panic. Rubber boots were flying off the shelves. They had interviewed several people who had gotten drenched running from the subway to their office.

"They think *they* have it bad," I said.

Rita was ignoring the TV in favour of reading ahead in her guidebook. A few minutes later, she looked up and said, "A lot of people get really depressed when they reach Santiago. They have such high expectations of the Camino that they believe their lives will change completely and that lifelong questions will be miraculously answered."

"How about quandaries? Will quandaries be cleared up?" I asked.

"Maybe not," said Rita.

"*Takane no hana*," said Fujiko.

"Flower on high peak," I translated. "Fujiko-*san*, it is a lovely thought, but I think something is lost in translation."

"Everybody believes their wish is special. Everybody want their wish come true," said Fujiko.

"People want to be the one-in-a-million pilgrim whose life changes," added Rita. "And some people's lives do change."

"As much as I love you both," I said, "If your lives change and mine doesn't, I'm going to have to find other friends because, at that point, I will be a loser and you will both be winners. And as a loser, I'm sorry, but I will not be caught dead with winners."

AFTER SIX MORE HOURS of walking through heavy rain, the sky began to clear. Rita looked ahead at the horizon where a glorious sliver of blue sky edged popcorn-like clouds out of the way. A town that we presumed to be Arzúa glowed brightly just beyond a ridge, a valley, some woods and a network of highways.

"Another 90 minutes to go," said Rita optimistically.

We headed into another dark wooded area and eventually emerged onto hillsides covered with neatly placed homes and manicured lawns. Manual farm equipment, namely ox ploughs like the ones we had watched being worked by farmers weeks earlier, decorated the suburban lawns of folk who paid tribute to the roots they would never return to. What had been a way of life on the Meseta turned to kitsch as we neared the 45-km mark. The streets and sidewalks were city-like, and wherever the countryside might have felt authentic, it turned out to be a bluff betrayed by heavy traffic, roaring by on the other side of strategically planted hedges.

Joining the hundreds of pilgrims walking the minimum 100 km to Santiago were locals who park in municipal lots and head into these managed parklands for a relaxing stroll. They were too focused on their own needs to shed city stresses to notice us. And many did not even say hello. As for *Buen Camino*, that greeting fell out of fashion after Sarria. The new recruits almost never said it, and we veterans had slipped into the more casual *Hola* instead.

ARZÚA WAS A TOWN that stretched along a modest ridge. We followed the main road toward our hotel on the opposite end of town. It occurred to me repeatedly that this was our second to last hotel before we would walk into Santiago on Sunday. I felt some anticipation along with a certain dread. I hadn't set any real goals for reaching Santiago, and I could feel some of the emptiness Rita had talked about.

Would my life change? Did I believe it should?

As I walked past the many shops lining the main street, I reviewed these questions and concluded that I was a man of very little faith. I refused to believe in God, yet I was not convinced that I was an atheist (I do, after all, capitalize the word God).

I did believe in one thing though: that it was impossible to believe in nothing. Beyond my capacity to critically think through everything, there lay a bedrock of assumptions that supported me.

And yet, at least to me, God was just a three-letter word to describe the unfathomable source of everything for which I was grateful. At the very least I wanted a bigger word. Something longer. And maybe in Spanish, ending in *"encia"*. Something that would fully capture the majesty inherent in a creator and subsequent administrator of absolutely everything.

To define God too clearly, it seems to me, is to claim to know more than we know – to know the unknowable, in fact.

Experience is my religion and what I believe in most. I tend to find answers floating amidst emotions conjured by stepping from stone to stone across a stream or walking along a rainy wooded path.

Maybe that's why I was on a Catholic pilgrimage years after leaving the church. Maybe I was on the Camino because at the age of 43, I hadn't decided exactly where I wanted my life to take me. At least with the Camino, that decision had already been made and I just had to follow the shells. Walking to Santiago was a lot easier than deciding what to do with my real life. In two days I would arrive at the finish line, with or without that question answered.

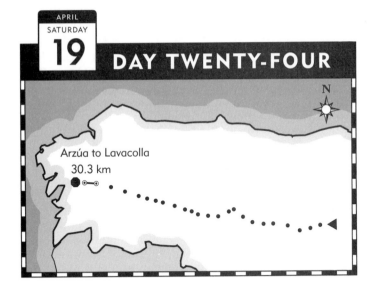

BREAKFAST WAS SERVED in the hotel bar, where three local university students were starting their day drinking beer and smoking cigarettes. When we entered, they squealed as though we were celebrities like Madonna, Prince and Yoko Ono. I couldn't tell if it was mockery or adulation, so I led Fujiko and Rita to a remote table by the windows, away from our fans. But rather than leave us alone, the students came over and chanted something in Spanish between fits of unrestrained laughter.

Between their exuberance and their Spanish, I was unable to understand what they were saying. I asked their ringleader, a short-haired woman named Celina, to write it down in my notebook:

> Caminante no hay camino,
> se hace camino al andar.
> ~ Antonio Machado

With help from Fujiko's electronic translator and my *Collins Spanish Phrase Book & Dictionary*, I wrote down what I believed they were saying:

Hey dude walking, there is no Camino.
You create the Camino by walking.

"There is no Camino? It's a little late to be telling us now," said Rita.

«¿*Qué*?» asked Celina.

«¿*Donde* were you *quando* start-*ábamos* in Burgos?» I asked.

«¿*Qué*?» repeated Celina.

"Where were you when we started in Burgos?" I repeated.

«*¡En Arzúa!*» replied Celina confusedly, «*¡Vivimos en Arzúa!*»

We laughed some more and I thanked them for their poem. But the idea that there was no Camino stayed with me.

Before leaving the bar, we kissed the air beside the cheeks of each of the three lively students three times and they did the same with each of us. Then we put on our ponchos and stepped outside into the steady rain. It was a lighter rain by far than the previous day, but the seemingly innocent drizzle would soak us to the bone.*

The rest of the morning, we zigzagged across the N-547 in moods drearier than the weather. To avoid getting depressed when the Camino ended the next day, we chose to be pro-active and suffer the loss immediately. The spitting mist was the perfect backdrop for this funk, which we endured mostly in silence, broken by occasional sighs until lunch.

Around 1 p.m., having walked nearly 16 km through the dampness, we spotted a bar on the edge of the highway. Pilgrims filed in and out of the tiny building like trick-or-treaters all wearing the same lame costume. Inside, 30 of us had squeezed into a space no bigger than an apartment-sized living room. We stood three deep at the bar, each vying for an opportunity to order a sandwich and a drink. As our turn arrived, a tour bus pulled up and emptied a fancier breed of pilgrim into the mix, one that expected immediate service. Fujiko,

---

* We did get soaked to the bone by the way. Those newfangled fabrics may well be waterproof. (To suggest otherwise would surely be a sue-able offence.) But let's just say that on day twenty-four, I would not recommend building a boat out of them, and leave it at that.

Rita and I stood next to a coat tree by the wall and waited for a free table.

A table cleared at the same time as our food arrived. "The gods are with us," I said, as we were served three glorious cheese sandwiches. The waiter returned with the two large beers and a glass of apple cider we had also ordered.

"Here's to us," said Rita, as she offered up a toast. "It has been a privilege walking with you both."

Rita's words had me and Fujiko return the same gratitude, which was as strong as our calf muscles had become and as sure as the rain that had pelted us, on and off, for the past 24 days.

BACK OUTSIDE, the grey loomed unchanged. We backtracked along the highway for 100 metres and then turned left to re-enter the forest. Two kilometres later, we arrived at the official 20-km marker, defaced, once again, by someone who had scribbled: *www.bahai.org*.

"What is it with the Bahá'í?" I asked. "Why can't they get their own signs?"

"You feel pretty strongly about this," said Rita.

"Well, look at it," I said. "What were they thinking when they defaced this marker?"

"Maybe you should write a letter," said Rita.

And so I wrote the following letter in my notebook:

Dear www.bahai.org,

I am happy that you have a religion.

We should all be so lucky to have something to give us solace in a confusing world. That you are true believers makes me happy for you. It really does.

But do you really hope to inspire devotion by spray-painting your website all over the Camino? I'd be more curious about your religion if it wasn't so preoccupied with defacing mine.

Sincerely,

Paul Huschilt (The Reluctant Pilgrim)

At the 16.5-km marker, Rita took a picture and said, "Sixteen and a half kilometres is less than a regular day of walking."

At the 13.5-km marker, I suggested that it might be a good idea to have a plan for our arrival.

"Sorry, but I have not stayed in the same place for more than 16 hours in the last 24 days," said Rita. "Planning what to do for more than one day in a row seems completely impossible to me."

At the 12-km marker, we arrived at the Santiago International Airport where we stood at the end of the runway and watched two jets take off and another one land. There were no houses in sight, despite several ranges of hills that spread out in front of us. Ironically, the woods surrounding the airport were some of the most untouched parcels of land we had seen in two days. Here, just 12 km from the Cathedral of Santiago, we could pretend we were somewhere much more remote. But 75 metres later we stepped back into civilization as we crossed the underpass of the N-634a and had to dodge traffic. As we arrived in Lavacolla, we were met with that day's only downpour. Rather than walk through it, we sat in a bus shelter for 20 minutes and had to wave on two bus drivers who were determined to help us against our will. Fujiko eventually led the way down a hedgerow to Hotel Garcas (☆), which was our final stop on the Camino.

"The last night is the traditional night to drink," said Rita.

"Uh-oh. Were we supposed to abstain until now?" I asked.

"No, it's just that this is the night to really party," she said. "In fact, I read in my guidebook that the song *Frère Jacques* [or *Brother John* in English] was first sung to a French monk who drank so much on his last night before Santiago that they couldn't wake him the next morning, the only morning that really mattered!"

"I have no problem drinking," I said, "As long as you'll sing me awake tomorrow."

At Hotel Garcas (☆), we found our pod-like rooms down a maze of twisted hallways. We washed our clothes, drank, ate and reminisced, and then spent 15 minutes trying to convince the receptionist to let us pay for our accommodations separately. It developed into the biggest knock-down argument of the entire Camino. Just when it seemed that we would have to phone our respective prime ministers to resolve the conflict, Fujiko offered to pay for all of us.

Both Rita and I chimed in that this wasn't right. "Sometimes wrong is right," said Fujiko handing the receptionist her husband's credit card.

That night, as I lay awake in bed, I thought about what the young people told us in the bar that morning. Maybe I'm in Spain to learn a lesson. If there is no Camino until I walk, I have no choice but to walk because my future depends on it.

My spine stiffened a little as if I was readying to help creation along – the creation of my own life. It wasn't that I thought I was solely responsible or in control of it all, it's that if I was playing the lead role in my own drama, I should at least take an interest in the play.

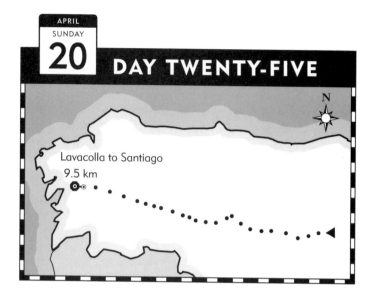

Lavacolla to Santiago
9.5 km

"THIS IS IT," SAID RITA, as she clicked on her head-mounted Mount Fuji flashlight and stepped into the darkness of the hotel parking lot at 6 a.m, with Fujiko and me following behind. We wove through suburban streets, climbed ancient stone steps past a small church, crossed a metal bridge through a stand of pine trees and then stepped momentarily into a pastoral Camino that would soon be citified. The dawn's first light formed a thin layer at the horizon that instantly converted black to grey.

Just before 8 a.m. we arrived at San Marco, a suburb with a quaint military feel. The seemingly fortified offices of TV2, the local television station, stood across the street. The early morning sun cast a forgiving light on its industrial harshness and somehow made it look appealing.

After about a kilometre through a no-man's-land during which we repeatedly asked "Are we on the right path?", the road suddenly curved and we approached the famous Monte Gozo, where pilgrims get their first glimpse of the cathedral.

Up above, there was an infinitely strange atmosphere. Storm clouds in the east and west glowed with equally eerie luminescence. The sun was behind one of the clouds, lighting it up, while also projecting enough light over its puffy frame to make the clouds opposite shine too. It was as though, on our arrival day, heaven and earth had joined forces to create one sunrise with two suns, each vying to cast a light over the cathedral that was more spectacular than the other.

"Just so you know, I will probably cry when I see the cathedral," said Rita.

"Me too," said Fujiko.

"Are you kidding, I'm planning on a total meltdown," I said. Fujiko handed us each a tissue from her jacket pocket as we circled the monument and looked out at the city to the west.

"Where is it?" I asked.

"It is behind those 12 cedars," exclaimed Rita, as she pointed to a distant stand of trees that hid all but the uppermost tip of one spire. We gasped at the sight that our aching bones had longed to see over the past 25 days. Our much-anticipated breakdowns began.

"The tip of the cathedral tower is so beautiful," whimpered Rita.

"Except it might just be one of the cedars," I said, as I wiped a tear from my eye.

"This is how I imagine it," snivelled Fujiko.

The eastern sun rose over the hill and a golden ray caught the stand of cedars and revealed without a doubt that the 13th point was indeed one of the three ornately carved spires of Santiago de Compostela Cathedral.

"Someone should cut down those trees," I said.

"It would certainly help the view," said Rita.

"If I see church better, I cry more," added Fujiko.

We stood and watched what little of the cathedral was visible for another minute or so and then Rita put her arms around our shoulders. "Better keep moving," she said. There was a lot of affection in her touch. As she herded us to the cathedral, I couldn't help but think how we'd become her special sheep and she'd become our favourite shepherd.

AS WE AGAIN TOOK TO THE ROUTE, we passed the Xunta Hostel Complex, boasting an astounding 800 beds. Then we followed the *Rúa de Peregrino* and crossed the sprawling E-1 before entering a tangle of throughways and buildings that began to coalesce into a denser city core.

There had been no arrows or scallop shells for more than 20 minutes, and the cathedral had begun to feel like a needle in a haystack. We followed an ornate stone path that was so artfully made we thought it had to be the Camino, but it snaked up a hill past several swank corporate headquarters before it stranded us in front of the Santiago Sports Stadium.

"Ah, the temple of Spain's other great religion – soccer," I said.

"This is crazy," said Rita, who was clearly put out. "They mark the Camino all the way to Santiago, then they just desert you."

Fujiko removed her pack and scurried about like a hound hell-bent on retrieving the scent. Rita took out her guidebook. As she read and reread the page on Santiago for hidden clues, I spotted a five-star hotel down the street and headed there. Inside, the handsome young man at reception seemed to be expecting me. He placed a large tourist map on the counter, spun it several times as he oriented himself and then scratched a large X to show where we were. Then he traced a long ragged line to the cathedral.

«Muchos gracias», I said. «Esteis muy amable».

«Buen Camino», he replied. And I returned to my rightful pilgrim's place in the dripping rain outside, where Rita and Fujiko were waiting.

"We have to go back that way," we all said in unison.

Map in hand, we skirted the soccer stadium and then continued along the *Rúa de Sán Lazaro*. We saw no shells anywhere; not on buildings, benches, trees, or roads or even on the children that passed. Eventually we did spot one on a sewer cover and we continued on with a warm and fuzzy feeling for the local sanitation department.

Then, a little later, pointing to a giant stone staircase, Fujiko exclaimed, "A yellow arrow!"

We followed it to the bottom, only to discover it led to more businesses that wanted our money. There ought to be a law against pulling pilgrims off the path, I thought to myself.

Rita led the charge back up the stairs and then onto a small street that changed its name practically from block to block. One second it was *Rúa do Home Santo*, then it became *Rúa de Rosario* and, a little later, *Rúa de San Domingo de Bonaval*. After about 10 minutes along this indecisive lane, we crossed a treed plaza, stepped across a street and entered the medieval core of Santiago.

"We are very close now," said Rita, with contained glee. Along roads too narrow to catch a glimpse of the cathedral in the distance, we walked blind and entered yet another plaza. As we continued along *Rúa da Acibichería*, the narrow stone street suddenly reverberated with a great tintinnabulation of church bells.

"St. James welcome us!" cried Fujiko in response to the ringing of bells that rolled down the street like an invisible red carpet meant just for us.

As we stepped into yet another square, we looked heavenward in anticipation of an inexplicably wondrous sight. We were met instead with the weathered facade of a stone church, overgrown in places with moss and lichen.

"Is that it?" I asked.

"I think it must be the back of the cathedral," said Rita. "But jeez, it doesn't look like much."

"Maybe it is pilgrim entrance," said Fujiko.

Instead of crying as I imagined I would, I laughed. I laughed at the absurdity of arriving at the back door of the great cathedral instead of the front. I laughed at the magic of the bells that chimed at the precise moment of our arrival. I laughed at walking 505.2 km with no clear goal, aim or ambition except to finish, and it was now over.

In spite of wanting to cry, I laughed. I felt too happy to weep. But somewhere in the back of my mind, the fact that I could not pinpoint what exactly I was happy about made me feel uneasy. I felt like a pretender.

Just next to us, a lone pilgrim was leaning on his stick, as unmovable as any pilgrim monument we passed on the Camino. Now that he had no place to go, he looked lost.

RITA LED US ALONG THE BUILDING, past two chatty police-men and through a great stone arch until we emerged into the main square. Pilgrims milled about aimlessly in small cliques. Their faces were as open and excited as children on the first day of summer vacation, before they realized how much time they were going to have to fill to not be bored silly until the fall. The pilgrims stood or sat in colourful clumps and looked up at the cathedral. Though it was still raining, most had removed the hoods to their ponchos to get the best view possible.

"Look – Dolores from Hamburg and her husband Helmut!" exclaimed Fujiko, suddenly waving madly before running toward them across the square.

Dolores waved back and then began to run toward Fujiko with equal speed. In a surreal moment, reminiscent of a love scene from a B-movie, two ponchos, one green, the other yellow, ran toward each other with arms outstretched.

Rita and I ran as well, and I realized it was the first time I had run in 505.2 km. It felt so good that I ran in circles around Fujiko and Dolores as they hugged like high-school girls at graduation. I ran across the square to Helmut, who approached at a more sober pace, and then ran back to circle Rita and Dol-ores as they hugged with genuine affection. I ran past pilgrims who looked open, happy and exhilarated, and past others that looked more confused, sad and without a destination.

Rita, Fujiko, Dolores and Helmut laughed at my antics, but in truth, other pilgrims acted up in the square as well. The plaza was a bubbling sea of activity, buoyed by the whole spectrum of heightened human emotions. Each of us felt something dif-ferent. But however our feelings may have differed, we shared one thing in common: we had lost our purpose.

Tomorrow, we would have to find something else to do.

I looked up at the steeples adorning the front of the cath-edral. They loomed in relief against bits of white clouds and blue sky. Immediately, I thought of my grandmother, Grace, who had just passed away. On days like this, she would ask if there was enough blue sky to make a Dutchman a pair of pantaloons. If there was, it would clear up. Sadly, there wasn't. Not quite.

"Astounding," said Rita, as she looked up at the cathedral's spectacular 18th century facade, which was decorated with two of every architectural curlicue known to man. At the very top, a stony St. James proudly looked on, holding his shepherd's staff as if to say, "Job well done." And throughout countless nooks and crannies, lesser saints waved discreetly, like religious royalty. Wherever they could get a foothold (which was almost everywhere), moss and flowering plants peeked out, making the great Santiago Cathedral look as if it would be just as at home in a soggy South Asian jungle.

Rita, Fujiko and I stood shoulder to shoulder. As lost as I was for what to do at this point, I felt sure about one thing: I was happy to have arrived.

"Is it a coincidence?" asked Fujiko.

"Is what a coincidence?" asked Rita.

"Is it coincidence that we live at same time as people we love?"

WE FOUND THE PILGRIM OFFICE by continuing on to the far end of the square and going around the cathedral, and then through a couple of streets. We stepped inside *Casa do Deán* and climbed a great stone staircase, where we had unobstructed views of the heads of pilgrims milling about in the lobby below. In the office upstairs, we took our place in line and waited more or less patiently for our "Pilgrim Certificates of Completion."

Just ahead of us, a group of seven Spanish sexagenarians handed their pilgrim passports across the counter to a young woman who flipped through them as stone-faced as if she worked for immigration. The pilgrim officer checked the stamps to see where they had stayed, calculating how far they walked each day. She bent ever closer over each passport for more careful inspection.

When she was done, she slapped the pilgrim passports back on the counter, shook her head and said «*Perdón, pero no se capacita. Próximo*». ("Sorry, but you don't qualify. Next.")

Though visibly upset, the lone man among the seven Spanish sexagenarians replied calmly that there must be some mistake. The pilgrim officer looked genuinely disappointed and assured him there was not. The pilgrim leaned forward and unleashed a volley of vowels laced with sibilance.

The pilgrim officer opened one of the passports and spoke slowly, as if she was explaining something to an imbecile child.

«*De Sarria a Pontmarín: 22,9 kilometros*.

«*De Pontmarín a Melide: 41,4 kilometros*.

«*De Melide a Lavacolla: 44,4 kilometros*.

«*De Lavacolla a Santiago: 9,5 kilometros*».

«*Si*», said the Spanish sexagenarians.

«*¡Imposible!*» said the officer.

«*Pero, si*».

«*Pero, no*».

«*¡Pero, Si!*»

«*¡Pero, No!*»

«*¿¿¿¿PERO QUÉ, PERO NO????*» they cried in unison.

«*¡Pero!*» said the pilgrim officer, matter-of-factly, before rattling off a rapid fire of local dialect sceptically, as she pointed at several of them in turn.

"What did she say?" asked Rita.

"I'm only guessing," I said, "But I think she said there is no way in hell that they walked 41.4 km one day and 44.4 km the next because that one is super-sized, that one has the plague and their combined age is older than the Camino."

"Don't point," said Rita, turning red as she looked away.

«*Han viajado en auto*», said the pilgrim officer to the seven Spaniards.

"You travelled by car," I translated quietly for Rita and Fujiko.

«*No*».

«*Autobús*».

«*No*».

«*Auto & autobús*».

«*No*».

«Taxis».

«No».

«Auto & taxis».

«No».

«¡Motocicletas!» exclaimed the pilgrim officer as if she had suddenly figured out their trick.

«¡¡¡Hemos caminado!!!» said the group of seven Spanish sexagenarians.

"They just said they walked," I translated.

«¡Imposible!» said the officer.

«Pero, si».

«Pero, no».

«¡Pero, Si!»

«¡Pero, No!»

«¿¿¿¿PERO QUÉ, PERO NO????»

Rita looked at the group. "There is no way they walked it," said Rita, totally unconvinced.

"Pilgrim lying?" asked Fujiko.

"I think so," said Rita. Fujiko shook her head.

The officer said something that stopped them in their tracks.

"What did she say this time?" asked Rita.

"It sounded to me like she said, 'There is no way you walked it because you are as fat as my uncle's drunken goat and as lame as his incontinent dog.' I might not have it exactly right, but I think I caught the gist. Staying abreast in a foreign language is all about stepping back and interpreting the gestalt."

The group of seven Spanish sexagenarians shook their fists collectively and stumbled out in a passionate Hispanic huff. Without missing a beat, the pilgrim officer called us to the counter with a congenial smile. She took a moment to inspect our *credencials*, stamped the oversized pilgrim office seal of St. James, nodded and smiled broadly.

«¡Enhorabuena!» she said.

"Uh-oh," said Fujiko.

"What does *la la la buena* mean?" asked Rita.

"Congratulations!" I answered reassuringly.

The pilgrim officer filled out three certificates of completion, writing out Latin versions of our names (*Paulum, Ritam* and *Fujikam*). Then she rolled each certificate, inserting them into cardboard tubing and asked us for an extra €2 each for the extra packaging.

As we proceeded back down the stairs, we proudly held up the certificates to our chests. Then we returned to the street just as a limousine parked on the sidewalk across from us. A uniformed driver got out and solemnly opened the back door. Rob emerged from the dark interior, followed by Alexandra. Next, the two young Austrian women stepped out. And several moments later, the two Swiss women, whom we repeatedly saw getting lost, emerged as well.

"We walked as far as we could today and then Alexandra called our driver," explained Rob.

"We picked up friends along the way," added Alexandra.

After hugs and air kisses, we said goodbye, as they entered the pilgrim office to make their case for certification too.

WE ENTERED THE *PLAZA DE PRATERÍAS*, which bordered the cathedral. In front of an ornate statue of bronze horses that jumped playfully out of cascading waters, we paused for a moment.

"Is Paul-*san* happy to walk Camino?" asked Fujiko.

I took in the dance where water and metal hooves met, and then nodded my head.

"Are you the one-in-a-million pilgrim whose life has changed?" asked Rita.

"I'm not so sure about that. But I am less interested in arguing with life. I just want to live it more."

"How?"

"By accepting it as it is. And trying to make a difference."

After a few moments, I asked Rita, "What about you? Did you find what you were looking for?"

"Absolutely. But I can't exactly put it into words."

"*Ganbatte kudasai*," said Fujiko. "Please try."

After another long pause, during which we stared at the fountain again, Rita said, "I believe more than I did before: both in God and in myself. How about you, Fujiko?"

"I walk for peace. And have peace in heart," said Fujiko. "*Dai manzoku*. I am so-o-o-o satisfied."

"What should we do now?" asked Rita.

"Walk," I said.

AS WE RETURNED TO THE MAIN SQUARE, I was surprised at how at home I felt. I looked up at St. James perched high on the facade of the cathedral, surrounded by untold architectural thingamajigs. I couldn't help but feel that I belonged here. It was as though walking 505.2 km had earned me the right to pitch a tent for the night or linger forever.

"We still have about an hour until the Pilgrim Mass at noon," said Rita. "In the meantime, I suggest we find a hotel."

"I want to stay at the best one available," I said without missing a beat.

"That would be the Parador," said Rita.

"Where is it?" I asked.

"Look left," said Fujiko.

"It's a palace," I exclaimed, as I took in the imposing facade of the Parador sitting kitty-corner to the cathedral.

"How many stars?" I asked.

"More than five," said Rita.

"Hallelujah!" I squealed.

The rain began to fall again as Rita and Fujiko headed down the hill to look for hotel rooms that did not involve a second mortgage. As for me, I headed straight for the Parador (☆☆☆☆☆☆).

About an hour later, we met up again in the square. The time was 11:55 a.m., and the Pilgrim Mass was set to begin in just five minutes.

"How is Paul-*san*'s room?" asked Fujiko.

"Oh, you know – It's okay," I said.

"Our hotel is great," said Rita. "I have my own terrace with a view of the cathedral."

"And I can see cathedral when I stick my head through skylight," added Fujiko.

"How much?" I asked.

"Only 70 euros," said Rita.

"Amazing," said Fujiko.

"How much to sleep with Henry the Eighth?" asked Rita, pointing at the Parador.

"Six times that," I said.

Rita and Fujiko looked at me like I had gone mad.

"You had better have that room with the balcony," said Rita, pointing to a balcony that spanned 30 feet, with French doors so grand you would expect the Pope to step out at any moment, with Queen Elizabeth II on his arm.

FUJIKO, RITA AND I followed the church-going crowd to Mass. We stepped up the stone staircase that climbed this way and then that, before reaching a high terrace that offered an imperial view of the square. The main entranceway to the cathedral was sealed, so the throng of pilgrims, tourists and worshippers formed a queue near a small entranceway where professional beggars frisked us like airport security. A young man, tall and thin and wearing a drab grey poncho, pulled an American couple aside to tell them how his money and passport were stolen after walking to Santiago from France. The man was obviously conning them. The American removed a €20 bill from his wallet and handed it to the man who smiled and then ushered the couple back in line as if to say, "You're free to go."

Inside, the air was stale and musty. We filed noisily into the darkness of the nave, dwarfed by massive stone pillars. Up front, the spectacular altar shone golden. A nun stood at the lectern, bathed in a dazzling beam of light that shone from the great domed apse above the central transept of the church. She had to repeatedly shush the crowd.

The Pilgrim Mass was competing with a constant press of pilgrims noisily circling the outside walls of the nave, performing the traditional rituals pilgrims complete upon arrival. These included placing a hand on the Tree of Jesse, knocking heads with Maestro Mateo, hugging the Golden Apostle behind the high altar and kneeling before the tomb of St. James, who is buried in the basement.

After the nun completed the congregational call and response, one of the eight priests who had been lounging in his fancy plush red chair stood to officiate Spain's most celebrated service. Rita, Fujiko and I elbowed our way through the crowd of those standing next to the seated congregation and found a tiny spot where we could lean against one of the great pillars and watch the Mass.

The priest appeared to be really on form, but most of what he said was impossible for us to decipher. The Gospel stood out, though. It was John 14:6. *Yo soy el Camino.* (I am the way.)

After the collection and offering, the priest approached the lectern and smiled out at us for some time. Then he read the list of pilgrims to be blessed for arriving in Santiago that day, first by naming the city where they had started their journey on the Camino, and then the number of pilgrims by country.

«*De Saint-Jean-Pied-de-Port: cuatro de España, tres de Alemania, uno de Finlandia, dos de Austria.*

«*De Roncesvalles: nueve de España, dos de Italia, dos de Francia, dos de Canadá.*

«*De Pamplona: una de Australia, uno de Irlanda, tres de Corea, dos de Estados Unidos de América.*

«*De Burgos: Diez de España, dos de Suiza, cinco de Alemania, uno de Irlanda, dos de Canadá, una de Japón.*»

"That is us!" cried Fujiko. Our eyes welled up as we leaned into each other and against the pillar.

The priest continued until he reached the town of Sarria, which marked 100 km – the least a pilgrim can walk and still be mentioned (albeit namelessly) in the great cathedral.

As the Mass continued, our attention wavered. Rather than struggling to understand the priest and follow the nun, we scanned the crowd and began to see people that we had met along the way.

"The Germans!" whispered Rita.

"Ronald from Korea," whispered Fujiko.

"The bald Spanish businessman," I pointed out.

"The snoring Irishman," said Rita.

"Heraclio and Fabían," I said, spotting them further back.

"Rob and Alexandra," said Fujiko.

"And the entire contents of his limo," I added, spotting the Swiss women and the Austrians too.

At the end of the Mass, the priest blessed us and the nun led us in song. As the members of the crowd stood to leave, the priest approached the lectern and made an announcement. Twelve men dressed in burgundy coveralls stepped onto the altar and a great silver urn was lowered from the apse.

The crowd gasped – one giant gasp that rustled through the musty air of the cathedral.

Excited whispers of «¡El Botafumeiro!» twittered through the crowd like birdsong.

Fabían and Heraclio led the rush to the altar, Heraclio's toe miraculously healed. The crowd pressed tightly behind them.

Rita turned to me, smiling, and said, "Showtime."

Suddenly, the immense pipe organ sounded out five deafening chords in a minor key, followed by a ghostly quiet rill of quick and eerie runs. The nun's voice, pleasant, familiar and slightly metallic, joined in. Two of the men dressed in burgundy reached out and steadied the great censer. A third man lit it and a musky smoke was set free, the cathedral all but electrified with the buzz of the crowd. Nine of the men dressed in burgundy pulled on the giant rope and hoisted the *Botafumeiro* about six feet above the floor of the sanctuary. One of the three closest to the censer reached up and grabbed it. He pushed the *Botafumeiro*, as though pushing a child on a swing. Then the nine men pulled on ropes again, causing the *Botafumeiro* to swing from side to side in ever-increasing arcs until it all but hit the roof, high overhead. On the downward swings, as the *Botafumeiro* plummeted, it narrowly missed the heads of pilgrims who looked up with three parts delight and one part terror.

I watched, leaning against the pillar with my friends, as the *Botafumeiro* swung upward for hundreds of feet and then careened toward the photo-snapping crowd like an angry comet on a leash. Arms outstretched, people snapped photos with their cellphones, unwittingly exposing their collective sweaty armpit odour to the curative musky smell of incense leaking from the silvery *Botafumeiro* in wafts of grey prayer-like smoke. For several minutes, I watched the *Botafumeiro* swing

past hypnotically, this way then that, this way then that, mesmerizing the masses. The rapid shotgun fire of cellphone flashes was incessant, as though the cathedral was housing a tremendous fireworks display. In all my years, this was the closest the Roman Catholic Church had ever come to matching the Technicolor wonder of Disney. I watched reservedly and at a distance, like a sensible adult who dares not jump in completely, or risk everything, but who longs to be a part of it all and to live the excitement wholly – even if only from the fringes.

"That was 240 euros well spent," announced Rita several minutes later, as the music died down and the *Botafumeiro* returned to earth.

"It was," I agreed. "I could never have imagined the sound of a thousand joyous people gasping."

The priests, adorned in red-on-white robes, took a ceremonial recess, and the men dressed in burgundy tied the *Botafumeiro* to a pillar. "So pilgrims don't steal it," I said.

As the crowd dispersed, friends greeted friends with more hugs and tears. As the last of the priests disappeared into the sacristy, a cowgirl, played by a man in drag, sidled up to the rood (the large wooden cross that hangs at the entry to the chancel). A photographer orchestrated a shoot as a crowd of curious onlookers gathered in case the model was a celebrity like Lady Gaga. The spectacle lasted for about 10 minutes until the nun returned and asked us to please be quiet for the one o'clock Mass, not at all fazed by the photo shoot of the cowgirl and the crucifix.

I found this to be a bit of a circus and led the way back through the nave and out the front doors of the cathedral. As we squeezed past the beggars, we stepped onto the grand terrace and into another heavy downpour.

IN THE WHITEWASHED CAVE of a back room at the *El Gato Negro* (The Black Cat), pilgrims fraternized and celebrated together for one last time. We ordered endless rounds of tapas and ceramic carafes of red wine as we tugged at the edges of the afternoon until it began to fray and we could no longer deny that our Camino was unravelling. In spite of carrying on bravely in broken English and Pilgrim Spanish, somewhere around 5 p.m. a spirit entered the room and we knew our Camino had to end.

The Spanish people at the table next to us sang *Volare* with an earnestness that was lost on me. All I could think of was Sergio Franchi singing the 1970s Plymouth *Volaré* commercials. Still, I wrote a loose English translation of what I thought they were singing. It was as though a part of me desperately wanted to feel the same excitement they felt before it was over. I wanted to live the final moments of the Camino fully.

> To fly, oh oh
> To Sing, oh oh oh oh ...
>
> Into the blue of the painted blue sky
> I fly, fly ever so high.
> Buoyed by a song that will not be outdone,
> I glide gladly over the sun.
>
> Volare, oh oh
> Cantare, oh oh oh oh ...

They sang the same verse repeatedly and in rounds – this left me to wonder at its meaning each time.

> My joy soars high in the sky
> As the moon retreats by and by.

The young woman at the head of the table sang to the handsome young *Barcelonés* to her right. He sang back, as he held his return ticket for an evening flight on Spanish Air awkwardly in front of his chest. He seemed flattered, if not a little discomfited, by her unwieldy sobs, which escaped whenever she reached for the high notes.

The singing eventually died away and peels of laughter broke the tension. Stepping back from the tables, we clasped each other's hands and stared intently into each other's eyes to say goodbye. At first, I felt a sense of emptiness, carved out by all the walking. But slowly, an overwhelming sense of affection rose within me. I stood among strangers and I did not know what to do. The feeling didn't seem like my own, but it was intense and extremely real.

Was this what comes of walking for 25 days? A capacity to love in a way I never knew before? It was a mix of joy and sadness that together formed a kind of compassion for them as well as for myself. I felt an acute sense of love and loss for these strangers in my life, for the end of the walk, for the completion of this incredible experience, for the fact that soon I would step off this Camino and continue my own life alone and anew.

In the adjoining hallway, the servers chatted and laughed as they waited for us to clear out before they would reset the tables for the next round of pilgrims, who would be arriving shortly for dinner. To them, our melodrama must have been just one show in an endless run, whose matinees and evening performances played out exactly the same, day after day, with alternate casts.

We left the restaurant and headed back across the square, where the lanky beggar leaned against the wrought-iron gate of the grand staircase to the cathedral. He ignored us now, choosing instead to take luxurious drags on his cigarette.

"WANT TO SEE MY ROOM?" I asked Fujiko and Rita.

"Of co-o-ourse!" said Fujiko.

A few steps further, a man trying to interest us in lodging stopped us and asked, «¿Para dormir?»

«¿Para dormir? ¡Parador!» I replied. ("To sleep? Parador!")

He smiled from ear to ear and gave me the thumbs up but then suddenly withdrew, as if to acknowledge that his own humble property couldn't possibly compare with the most famous hotel in Santiago.

The three of us continued across the square, as pods of newly arrived pilgrims stared daftly up at the bell towers. Happy squeals rang out from time to time as the pilgrims rec-ognized those they had met along the way. Local grandfathers criss-crossed the square pushing baby carriages, and students from *Colegio de San Jerónimo* travelling in nonchalant packs headed nowhere in particular, or hung out under the fixed gaze of St. James. We didn't see anyone we knew and so continued unimpeded past the bellhops standing outside and into the lobby of the Parador – the medieval palace that was my home away from home for only €420,11 a night.*

At the front desk, the staff bowed and smiled at me as if I was royalty. Then they nodded politely at Fujiko and Rita as if they were staff. I have arrived, I thought to myself.

I asked one of the porters to show us to my room because I didn't remember where it was. Built in 1499, the Parador was said to be the oldest hotel in the world. It was originally a pilgrims' hospital and, as in all hospitals, it was easy to get lost. Take one wrong turn and you could be spewed into one of the hotel's four cloisters, which lead to separate wards on the property that spans an entire city block. The hotel was so big that it was hard to remember where you came from. And it was littered with so many distractions – priceless antiques, statues, statuettes, paintings, Persian rugs, hanging tapestries, giant urns, knights in shining armour (minus the knights themselves), spectacular courtyard gardens, a concert hall, grand pianos (double-parked in places) and palatial dining facilities – that it was easy to forget where you were going.

When I passed other pilgrims in the corridors, I couldn't help but wonder if they were as lost as I was. Some of them looked like they had wandered for some time in search of their room.

"I can see how you could get lost in here," said Rita.

"Nothing a few arrows couldn't fix," I replied conspiratorially.

The bellhop was gruff but kind. He led us down a narrow hallway with tiny artefacts from the Camino encased in glass cabinets. He steered us into a windowless stone staircase: we twisted and turned up foot-worn steps to the third floor and reappeared at the edge of an arcade. He led us through some modern glass doors and we stepped into a foyer that appeared to belong only to my room. When we got to Room 301, he

---

* Approx. C$671.63 or US$667.23

turned a key and pushed the heavy, splendidly carved wooden doorway open, then flipped a switch that turned on every light in the place. Rita and Fujiko entered first. As I followed them, he handed me the key, nodded, and backed away.

"Paul-*san*, you are a king," said Fujiko.

"I prefer emperor," I said.

"Do we get a tour?" asked Rita.

"Sure, I guess," I said with feigned humility meant to hide how thrilled I was at being asked.

As we removed our shoes and placed them under one of two wooden benches, I saw that the staff had returned my boots, which they'd cleaned at my request. The boots shone like new. But when I looked more closely, I saw they'd been rubbed so completely that the fabric had frayed, leaving holes on each boot where toes should have met foot.

I could see that I would soon be saying goodbye to these friends, too – these friends that had sacrificed themselves for my Camino. They gave their lives for me on the 505.2 km walk, and sacrificed their soles so that I could traverse plains, mountains and rivers. They had supported me through the laughs, the tears, the frustrations and each small triumph. And now, renewed as they were, I could see that their Camino had ended, too. I would leave them behind in Spain and, for my trip home, would wear my mountain flip-flops. Their life, too, had all but ended, but I had a greater loyalty to them for having walked me to the top of Mount Fuji and back. I would toss them out only after I had returned home and stepped onto domestic soil.

Rita and Fujiko waited patiently for me to begin the tour. I started by pointing out the many paintings in the richly panelled front hall. "These paintings are representational without being photographic," I said. "They maintain a certain mystery and don't kill you with needless details. Now please follow me to the grand hall, which is 29 feet long by 15.5 feet wide."

"The ceilings are so high," said Fujiko, as she looked up and entered the main living area.

"At least 20 feet," I pointed out. Overhead, there were eight stars etched in relief between crosses of thick but finely carved wooden beams.

Fujiko noticed beside the living room a three-foot wooden carving of St. James, squatting yogi-style atop what appeared to be a 14th century TV cabinet. The saint had two fingers extended heavenward, mimicking San Froilán in Virgen del Camino.

"The thick Persian rug in the centre of the room would sleep 18 pilgrims easily," I said. In the centre of the rug stood a rectangular coffee table with short striped multi-coloured legs. It was stylishly dinged and damaged. The taupe sofa, which was the coffee table's *raison d'être*, boasted cushions stuffed so full they looked as if they would pop if you sat on them. Two high-back chairs looked as uncomfortable as they were glorious, and completed the sitting area with magazine-cover perfection.

Next, I turned my attention to the massive golden chandelier suspended over the coffee table.

"It has 31 flame-shaped bulbs!" I pointed out (having counted them earlier). "Eighteen in the outer ring and 13 in the inner one: 60 watts each!"

"Somewhere in Spain, there's a wind turbine spinning just for you," said Rita.

Suddenly I felt the need to resign as tour guide and enter the moment fully. Before I did, I looked up to assure myself that the chandelier's heavy chain emerged from one of the mighty beams that criss-crossed the ceiling and not from plaster that might crumble anticlimactically. Then, I stepped onto the sofa and onto one of two high-backed chairs that surrounded the coffee table, and stretched my arms overhead.

"Jump," cried Rita. "Swing!"

"It is very high," warned Fujiko.

But it was too late.

I leaped as carefree as I used to as a child when I would jump off the end of the dock at my grandparents' lake. I grabbed two sturdy spokes of the chandelier as I used to grasp at the heavy rope tied to the tired oak overhanging the sandy swim-ming area below. I swung, clinging to the light fixture at one end, while my skinny legs dangled like untied shoelaces. Rita, making sounds of delight, pushed intermittently at my legs, until I began to trace ever-growing arcs.

"It won't break," I said assuredly. "It's stronger than you think!"

My feet narrowly missed the gilded painting of a rural setting over the couch on one side and the straw-coloured wallpaper opposite. My lower back cracked audibly and I felt such freedom. I had come untethered from the dock. The ladies' arms were in the air. They squealed with delight. Light shifted. Breath. Freedom. They ducked and then pushed. In an instant, I felt the importance of implicating myself into my Camino until pilgrim and way were one.

Rita collapsed onto one of the hoity-toity chairs and Fujiko fell onto the sofa, both beside themselves with laughter. I let go, landing on the far side of the carpet on all fours. It took me several moments to return to the room.

FUJIKO AND RITA turned their attention to the huge writing desk at the far end of the space. It had three lamps made of marble and ornately carved wood. Each lamp was capped with a linen shade that rested at an odd angle. Rita sat herself at the desk and throne-like chair, which was upholstered in gold and baby blue brocade. "I feel like Queen Isabella," she said.

Over Rita's shoulder, there was a gargantuan oil painting of a naked child in the arms of a smiling woman dressed in red. They were surrounded by a suffering mob that seemed to be dying of the plague.

"Your public awaits you," I said, as I pulled back floral cream-and-gold floor-to-ceiling drapes to reveal an imperial set of French doors. Beyond the doors lay the stone balcony facing the cathedral. The balcony spanned the full length of the apartment. It was six feet deep and made of solid stone. "If I attached this to the side of my house in Toronto, my house would tip over," said Rita, duly impressed.

People in the square noticed us immediately. "They think I am the emperor's grandmother," said Fujiko, as she stood taller than normal and waved royally. For several minutes, we watched a tour bus empty its contents in front of the Parador. An older crowd poured out and filed into the hotel without so much as glancing over their shoulders at the cathedral. As it started to rain again and my own private gargoyles vomited rainwater onto the balcony from above, we headed back inside.

Then I led them across the room and opened a set of majestic wooden doors to reveal a giant canopied bed; I stretched the truth a little when I pronounced, "Napoleon once slept here."

"Wow," said Fujiko.

The bed's great straw yellow and baby blue striped tent was large enough to sleep an emperor and his entire army in the field with a sea of fluffy pillows to hide them in. "Wow!" said Rita.

"Can we jump on it?" asked Fujiko.

Before I could respond, they rushed past me and started bouncing on the bed like kids on a trampoline. (A very expensive antique trampoline.) "I hope it doesn't break," I said.

"Don't worry. I have husband's credit card."

Once out of breath, the ladies hopped off the bed and opened the door to the dressing area and hallway to the white marble bathroom. Fujiko opened and closed the doors to the clothes closets while Rita went through the baskets of amenities in the washroom. "You don't need this do you?" asked Rita, as she held up a bottle of women's perfume.

"Take this, too," I said and handed her a linen sack labelled *higiene feminina*. The bathroom was astounding, with five separate water features, three of which could be sat on or in.

"Where does this go?" asked Fujiko.

"That's the door to the entrance hallway, back where we started," I said, "The whole apartment forms a giant loop. Sixty-three laps makes one kilometre. I measured."

WE ORDERED IN A FORMAL TEA, which we took under the chandelier in the living room, and snacked on the same pastries we had on the Camino, only smaller and more expensive.

"What next?" asked Rita.

"Is it over?" I asked.

"Well, we made it."

"Paul-*san*, you are in Santiago now," said Fujiko.

After a long pause, I said, "From now on, I am going to walk more."

"Would you do it again?" asked Rita.

"Yes, but not necessarily here. I think I'll just walk in Toronto more."

"Why?"

"Because it helps me think. And it helps me stop thinking. It quiets my mind so that I can focus on simple thoughts that deserve my attention most, like gratitude."

THAT NIGHT, LYING IN NAPOLEON'S BED, I wondered if he might have actually slept in something similar when he planned his campaigns.

Outside, a bagpiper was busking in the alley. I turned on the lamp beside the bed and picked up the phone. I dialled the front desk and asked them to offer him €40 to play somewhere else. A few minutes later the music stopped. Twenty minutes after that, an accordionist took his spot.

The bells of the Santiago Cathedral rang every 15 minutes, and every hour.

As I began to doze off, I reviewed my latest adventures and searched for the moment when I gave in – when I finally decided to enjoy myself regardless of whether I wanted to walk to Santiago or not.

What is life, after all, but a pilgrimage that begins without our asking, and ends without our consent? While the walk is on, we might as well make the most of it.

«¡*Vamos Carlos!* ¡*Ole!*» cried a group of drunken students in the square.

And I fell asleep.

Paul's Fractional (Yet Complete) Pilgrimage

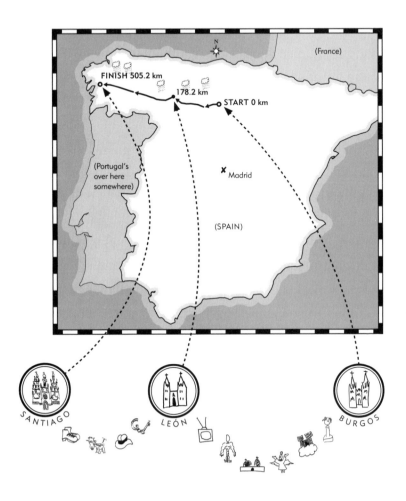

APPENDICES

APPENDIX A
Checklist of Things to Bring

What	Weight (grams)	Weight (pounds)	Why
Essentials			
Backpack (45 L)	1,905	4.2	Rollaway luggage won't work in the mountains.
500 mL bottle of water	1,070	2.36	To be refilled with beverage of choice.
Sleeping bag	850	1.87	Ultra-light and good to almost freezing.
Rain jacket	360	0.79	Lightest possible – lime green and grey.
Hooded rain poncho	280	0.62	Makes me look like an idiot.
Waterproof backpack cover	120	0.26	Without this, things would get soggy.
Spork	10	0.02	Plastic spoon, fork and knife, all rolled into one.
Shoes & Clothing			
Walking shoes	1,080	2.38	Waterproof.
Mountain flip-flops	585	1.29	My favourite old pair of hiking boots.
Two Merino wool long-sleeved pullovers	540	1.19	Cool when it's warm, warm when it's cool.
Convertible walking pants	325	0.72	Unzip legs to make shorts. Includes built-in underwear!
Convertible walking pants	350	0.77	One size bigger so I can overeat.
Two quick-dry t-shirts	280	0.62	They dry in the time it takes to have a shower.
Two pairs of lined running socks	130	0.29	With a trademarked anti-blister system.

What	Weight (grams)	Weight (pounds)	Why
Mount Fuji LED headlight	150	0.33	Straps to your head like a coal miner, field surgeon or electric cyclops.
Merino wool tights	120	0.26	Lighter than longjohns.
Sunhat	80	0.18	To keep Mission Control from burning up.
Two pairs of underwear	70	0.15	With the support pilgrims expect.
Featherweight pair of gloves	35	0.08	Spain isn't supposed to be cold, is it?
For Writing & Work			
ASUS Eee miniature PC and cords	1,022	2.25	Weighs only 2.25 lbs! To write, email and Skype.
Notebook, pen and marker	170	0.37	To record deepest thoughts and insights.
Waterproof wristwatch	70	0.15	What would an incomplete guide be without exact times?
Speaking engagement calendar	20	0.04	Photocopied and stored in spine of backpack to remind me that I do actually work for a living, and that I'll be speaking to audiences again when I go home.
Business cards (10)	5	0.01	In case I meet Oprah.
Toiletries etc.			
Toiletry travel case	45	0.1	A necessary evil – lightest I could find.
Bandages	40	0.09	Enough for an epidemic of blisters.
Shampoo (1 bottle)	30	0.07	Hotel size. I'll collect more along the way.

What	Weight (grams)	Weight (pounds)	Why
Toothbrush	25	0.06	Can't eat until I brush my teeth.
Toothpaste	25	0.06	See above.
Dental floss	20	0.04	Don't want to end up like Austin Powers.
Nail clippers	15	0.03	Nails grow only 0.19 cm/month – half the speed that the Himalayas are rising. Still, it's gross when they get too long.
Disposable razor	10	0.02	I'm a pilgrim, not a hippie.
Rubber tip stimulator.	10	0.02	Not what it sounds like – for teeth.
Miscellaneous			
Collins Spanish Phrase Book & Dictionary	165	0.36	With essential grammar pages 188–192.
Birth certificate	5	0.01	In case I die.
Health card	5	0.01	In case I don't die.
Total:	**10,022**	**22.07**	

APPENDIX B
Checklist of Things Not to Bring*

What	Weight (grams)	Weight (pounds)	Why Not
Winter coat	1,000	2.2	Make one out of sleeping bag – see Day 12.
Bath towel	150	0.33	Dry off with a t-shirt.
Digital camera	115	0.25	Draw instead.
Bathing suit	60	0.13	Swim naked or not at all.
House keys	50	0.11	Leave them under a pot by the back door.
Personal deodorant	40	0.09	On the road everyone stinks.
Shaving cream	30	0.07	Use soap instead, or toothpaste.
Driver's licence	5	0.01	Pilgrims don't drive.
Gym membership	5	0.01	Who needs a gym when you walk all day?
Total:	**1,550**	**3.2**	

----

* PLEASE NOTE: Suggestions only. Follow these guidelines at your own risk. For example, don't leave your winter coat, freeze to death and then blame me.

APPENDIX C
Day by Day

Day	From	To	Distance (km)
1	Burgos	Hornillos del Camino	18.8
2	Hornillos del Camino	Castrojeriz	21.2
3	Castrojeriz	Boadilla del Camino	19.1
4	Boadilla del Camino	Carrión de los Condes	26.6
5	Carrión de los Condes	Terradillos de Templarios	26.8
6	Terradillos de Templarios	Sahagún	13.2
7	Sahagún	El Burgo Ranero	18.8
8	El Burgo Ranero	Mansilla de las Mulas	14.7
9	Mansilla de las Mulas	León	19.1
10	León	Virgen del Camino	8.5
11	Virgen del Camino	Hospital de Órbigo	27.7
12	Hospital de Órbigo	Astorga	16.8
13	Astorga	Rabanal del Camino	21.4
14	Rabanal del Camino	Acebo	17.0
15	Acebo	Ponferrada	15.7
16	Ponferrada	Villafranca del Bierzo	24.5
17	Villafranca del Bierzo	Vega de Valcarce	19.7
18	Vega de Valcarce	O'Cebreiro	11.2
19	O'Cebreiro	Triacastela	20.7
20	Triacastela	Sarria	25.0
21	Sarria	Pontmarín	22.9
22	Pontmarín	Palas de Rei	26.1
23	Palas de Rei	Arzúa	29.9
24	Arzúa	Lavacolla	30.3
25	Lavacolla	Santiago	9.5
		Total:	**505.2**

APPENDIX D
Incomplete List of Where the Reluctant Pilgrim "Slept"

Day	Town	Accommodations	Contact
1	Hornillos del Camino	Municipal *Albergue*	947-411-220
2	Castrojeriz	*Puerta Del Munte* Hotel(☆☆)	947-378-647
3	Boadilla del Camino	En el Camino	979-810-284
4	Carrión de los Condes	Santa Clara Monastery	979-880-134
5	Terradillos de Templarios	Not sure – I was really sick	incomplete
6	Sahagún	Alfonso VI (☆☆)	987-781-144
7	El Burgo Ranero	Small hotel opposite the municipal *albergue*	incomplete
8	Mansilla de las Mulas	Municipal Albergue	987-310-138
9	León	Hotel Paris (☆☆☆) – (Room 202)	987-238-600
10	Virgen del Camino	No-name hotel	Look for sign in window of bar opposite church
11	Hospital de Órbigo	Parish Hostel	987-388-444
12	Astorga	Hotel Gaudí (☆☆☆)	987-615-654
13	Rabanal del Camino	*Refugio* Gaucelmo	987-691-901
14	Acebo	*La Trucha*	987-695-548
15	Ponferrada	Hotel Madrid (☆☆☆)	incomplete
16	Villafranca del Bierzo	Hotel Plaza (☆☆☆)	incomplete
17	Vega de Valcarce	El Recanto	987-543-202
18	O'Cebreiro	*Santuario do Cebreiro Hostal*	982-367-125
19	Triacastela	*Berce de Caminho*	982-548-127

Day	Town	Accommodations	Contact
20	Sarria	*Pension Pedra*	982-530-130
21	Pontmarín	Hotel Villajardín (☆☆)	982-545-252
22	Palas de Rei	You don't want to know	not recommended
23	Arzúa	Hotel Suiza (☆☆)	981-500-862
24	Lavacolla	Hotel Garcas (☆) Just don't try to pay separately	incomplete
25	Santiago	Parador (☆☆☆☆☆) (*Hostal de los Reyes Católicos*) (Suite 301 with balcony)	981-582-200

APPENDIX E

**How to Choose the Right Bed
for the Best Night's Sleep**

1. Sleep by a window. (You control the airflow.)
2. Sleep on an outside wall. (Less noise. More privacy.)
3. Sleep on the bottom bunk. (Not as far to fall. More places to hang laundry.)
4. Sleep far from doors and toilets. (Less noise. Fewer smells.)
5. Avoid the socially inept and talk-aholics.
6. Avoid those wearing too much perfume.
7. Avoid those not wearing enough perfume.
8. Avoid the sick and anyone who's caught the plague.

APPENDIX F
Sample Pilgrim Budgets*

Budget A – Albergues – Eating In (in euros)			
Item	Average	Days	Total
Albergues only	7	25	375
Eat-in meals	20	25	700
		Total:	1,075
		Add in *Botafumeiro*:	240
		Grand Total:	1,315

Budget B – Best Available Accommodations – Eating Out (in euros)			
Item	Average	Days	Total
Best available hotels	85	25	2,125
Restaurant meals	35	25	875
		Total:	3,000
		Add in *Botafumeiro*:	240
		Grand Total:	3,240

---

* Budgets are for illustrative purposes only, and do not include airfare, supplies or postcards. The point to consider is reserving the *Botafumeiro*. Why walk that far and not go all the way?

Hoity-toitiest Hotel:

Parador in Santiago/*Hostal de los Reyes Católicos* (☆☆☆☆☆)

981-582-200

www.paradores-spain.com/spain/pscompostela.html

Best Hotel Value in Santiago:

Hotel Pombal – Santiago (☆☆☆)

902-405-858

www.pousadasdecompostela.com

info@posadasdecompostela.com

Several rooms have private terraces or gardens facing the cathedral.

Best Bars:

Cowboy Bar – El Ganso

El Gato Negro – Santiago

Best View:

O'Cebreiro – even with the fog

Favourite Restaurant:

El Apostol

Cacabelos, C/ Santa María, 29, 24540, Cacabelos, León.

987–549-189

Best Complete Guidebook:

A Pilgrim's Guide to the Camino de Santiago

John Brierley, Camino Guides, 2008.

Best Spanish Phrase Book:

Collins Spanish Phrase Book & Dictionary

HarperCollins Publishers, Glasgow, 2004.

It's small and has a good grammar section. In blank spaces, I conjugated verbs I might have needed.

Best FREE Tip:

Whenever you visit a fruit and vegetable section of a grocery store pick up some of their FREE plastic gloves (offered for handling fruits and vegetables.) Whenever it's cold and rainy, wear these plastic gloves over your own. Use elastic band at wrist to keep them on.

ELASTIC
BAND

Smallest PC:

Asus Eee PC. 2.25 pounds. Under $500. Brilliant!

Biggest Argument:

Hotel Garcas (☆), Lavacolla

Best Plenary Indulgence:

Botafumeiro: €240.

To order, email peregrinos@archicompostela.org.

Best Moment:

Now

APPENDIX H
The Life of Buddha (Abridged)

The young Buddha was a model child, who became a typical teenager, believing He knew everything. Except in the Buddha's case, He really did. The Buddha mastered the arts and sciences without so much as lifting a brush or sharpening a pencil. He could speak 64 different languages, four more than what existed at the time. Even so, the Buddha went to school to please His father, the King.

"Son," said the Buddha's father. "In today's day and age, how can you expect millions of people to follow you if you don't have a degree?"

"You are right, father," said the Buddha, even though He knew he wasn't.

The Buddha had a very powerful mind. Through the power of meditation, He would sometimes shoot an arrow through 5 metal tigers. Other times He missed, but people never talk about that.

One day, when the Buddha saw common people suffering, He was so moved, He sat, crossed his legs and did nothing.

About 10 years later, when the Buddha was 29, He called his parents into his room where He was sitting and said," I want to move out and sit among the suffering people."

Buddha's mother, the Queen, whispered to the King, "Frankly, I think it is better than Him sitting around here all day doing nothing."

But the King said, "No!"

"You never let me do anything I want," cried the Buddha.

"I am the father in this house," said the King.

"But I am 29 years old," said the Buddha.

"And look what you have done with your life," said the King: "Nothing!"

"Your father *does* have a point," said the Queen.

The King did everything he could to keep the prince in the palace, including pizza, which only made the Buddha fatter. It did not however, soften the Buddha's resolve.

The King posted guards so the Buddha could not escape, so the Buddha went on and on about how all beings just want to be happy and avoid suffering, until the guards could not take it anymore and cried, "You are insufferable."

After that, the Buddha freed Himself through the servants' entrance.

The Buddha rode a horse to India where He found a suitable place for meditating under a Bodhi tree. For six long years, He sat and focused on "the ultimate nature of all phenomena." The next morning, the Buddha achieved perfect enlightenment. To celebrate, He crossed his legs the other way.

THE END

APPENDIX I
The Reluctant Pilgrim's 10 Biggest Lessons of the Camino

1. Not believing in facts doesn't make them any less real.
2. When you walk and walk, you learn that it really is a small world after all.
3. Sometimes chocolate and anchovies taste good together.
4. What happens on the Camino stays on the Camino – unless you write a book about it.
5. It's only when you walk your ass off that you know how far you can drag it.
6. The world would be a better place if we all wore built-in underwear.
7. Doing with nothing is easy provided you have enough.
8. What stands between me and making my dreams come true is me.
9. If every single high school student was sent to walk the Camino, war would be replaced with one great big party that we would have to clean up after.
10. If quantum physics is true and there really are 100 parallel universes, then we each carry within us the potential to swing from a chandelier at any given moment.

Reluctans Peregrinus

SACRUM TESTIMONIUM SUSTENTA DE PEREGRINATIONE ET PERFECTA

IN NOMINE regionis metropolitanae largae et extentae Santiago, (Toronto non excluso,) atque in spiritu totalis benevolentiae humanae totius orbis terraraum blah blah blah ...

Nunc hic peregrinus invitus, pulsus tamen propitiis zephyris, suo comiti peregrino praesentat et solemniter authenticas litteras in omni terra publicas confert proclamantes nominatim

_____.

INSERT YOUR NAME ABOVE

"Si peregrinus reluctans hoc perficere potest, tu ipse similiter..... Hodie incipe, (vel mañiana, si forte occupatus)."

Hoc testimonium his adstantibus confertur et praesentatur hoc

die _____, menis _____, anno _____.
    day   month   year

Canonicus deputatus pro reluctantibus peregrinis

X
_____
Reluctans Peregrinus

APPENDIX K
Walking Chart*

(The numbers represent the days of walking required to get from one city to a corresponding city on the chart, based on 20-km days.)

	Toronto	Ottawa	Quebec City	Iqaluit	Fredericton	Charlottetown	Halifax	St John's	Winnipeg	Regina	Yellowknife	Edmonton	Whitehorse	Victoria	Washington DC	New York	Chicago	Los Angeles
Toronto		18	36	117	52	66	63	106	76	102	153	135	204	169	28	28	35	175
Ottawa	18		19	104	35	49	48	89	84	111	154	142	207	179	37	27	52	190
Quebec City	36	19		95	18	31	32	70	97	123	160	153	214	192	50	35	71	208
Iqaluit	117	104	95		99	99	107	102	115	129	113	138	166	183	141	129	137	236
Fredricton	52	35	18	99		14	14	54	115	142	175	170	230	210	58	42	87	226
Charlottetown	66	49	31	99	14		9	40	127	153	183	181	238	222	70	53	101	239
Halifax	63	48	32	107	14	9		45	129	155	188	184	243	224	64	48	98	238
St John's	106	89	70	102	54	40	45		161	186	204	211	259	253	109	93	141	278
Winnipeg	76	84	97	115	115	127	129	161		27	87	60	87	95	100	103	58	123
Regina	102	111	123	129	142	153	155	186	27		73	35	110	69	126	130	81	107
Yellowknife	153	154	160	113	175	183	188	204	87	73		50	55	83	181	180	144	159
Edmonton	135	142	153	138	170	181	184	211	60	35	50		76	45	160	163	116	110
Whitehorse	204	207	214	166	230	238	243	259	87	110	55	76		78	231	231	189	160
Victoria	169	179	192	183	210	222	224	253	95	69	83	45	78		191	197	143	83
Washington DC	28	37	50	141	58	70	64	109	100	126	181	160	231	191		17	48	185
New York	28	27	35	129	42	53	48	93	103	130	180	163	231	197	17		58	197
Chicago	35	52	71	137	87	101	98	141	58	81	144	116	189	143	48	58		140
Los Angeles	175	190	208	236	226	239	238	278	123	107	159	110	160	83	185	197	140	

----

* Why fly to Spain for a pilgrimage, when you can walk to Chicago, LA, or New York City? If that sounds like too much, put down this book and walk to the corner and back. Get off the bus one stop early and walk the rest of the way home. Climb a flight of stairs. Go for a stroll (and buy a snack on the way if necessary). Ramble, traipse, trudge, tramp, or dawdle. Stride and stretch those legs. Mosey, just a tad, now and then. But by all means, perambulate. Why? Because it's good for the soul.